Praise for

FULLY ALIVE

"Rich with tools and guidance for how entrepreneurs can accomplish ambitious social missions by building thriving businesses."

—John Mackey, founder and CEO of Whole Foods Market

"We need new thinking to tackle the massive environmental and structural problems the world faces today. Tyler points a way forward, using ancient knowledge and practices, and lays a foundation for its application in modern business."

—Rose Marcario, CEO and president of Patagonia, Inc.

"A refreshingly honest, often brutally frank blend of big-picture inspiration and pragmatic learnings that will help inform any entrepreneur about facing and overcoming challenges."

—Gary Hirshberg, cofounder, chairman, and former CEO of Stonyfield Farm

"A crash course in the trials and tribulations—as well as the triumphs—of starting a social venture."

—Russ Siegelman, Stanford University professor; former partner and managing director, Kleiner Perkins Caufield & Byers; chairman of the Global Innovation Fund

"Tyler Gage represents a hope-inspiring new generation of social entrepreneurs who are proving that conscious business can be a powerful force for good."

—Paul D. Rice, cofounder and CEO of Fair Trade USA

"A compelling story of purpose, perseverance, patience, and partnership. Runa is an innovative and sustainable social business that is positively impacting the lives of countless indigenous people in the Amazon."

—Ann Veneman, former executive director, UNICEF, and former US Secretary of Agriculture

"In this powerful and riveting book, Tyler manages to achieve a rare combination of three distinct things: Vividly conveying an extraordinary hero's journey, while narrating a highly educational textbook about business and startups, and expressing a heartfelt, inspiring, no-holds-barred treatise on shamanic practices applied to a modern business. I could not put it down."

—José Luis Stevens, PhD, author of *The Power Path*

"Tyler Gage knows how to tell a story, and he has amazing stories to tell. Readers of *Fully Alive* will enjoy the journey. You'll discover that powerful answers to profound questions can be found in the most unexpected places."

—Doug Hattaway, founder and CEO, Hattaway Communications, and former advisor to Hillary Clinton and Al Gore

"A useful, thoughtful, and well-written book about how making your way through life, business, and the rainforest can all be a very similar enterprise."

—Mark Plotkin, PhD, cofounder and president, Amazon Conservation Team, and author of *The Shaman's Apprentice*

"Tyler's accomplishment as a young, visionary entrepreneur who has built a sustainable social enterprise has been an inspiration to our students. *Fully Alive* provides a comprehensive understanding for how to optimize social enterprise creation to generate business success while changing lives and sustaining incomes of vulnerable populations."

—Scott B. Taitel, clinical professor of Public Service and director of Impact, Innovation, and Investment, NYU Wagner

"*Fully Alive* is a great story of how curiosity, tenacity, a little naïvety, and a lot of personal growth can be the right recipe for launching a social enterprise. I thoroughly enjoyed the ride, from the hills of California, to the halls of Brown University, to the indigenous communities of the Amazon, to the boardroom in New York."

—Lauren Hattendorf, head of investments, Mulago Foundation, and lecturer at the Stanford Graduate School of Business

"*Fully Alive* offers many powerful lessons and tools across a range of topics, including leadership, ethics, and strategy—an excellent read for students, entrepreneurs, and anyone looking to embark on new ventures (or adventures!) in their life."

—Alan Harlam, director, Social Innovation, Brown University

"Runa's story illustrates that doing well by doing good is not simply a cliché. It was what motivated its founders in the first place, and is the basis of its continued great success."

—Danny Warshay, professor, executive director, Jonathan M. Nelson Center for Entrepreneurship, Brown University

"It's a refreshingly honest story of young entrepreneurs with a unique mix of social purpose, grit, and creative strategy."

—Tom First, cofounder of Nantucket Nectars and operating partner at Castanea Partners

"Exciting and inspirational. Tyler Gage paves the way for the future of business! Spiritual/travel adventure meets business manual—*Fully Alive* is as entertaining as it is a blueprint for the new wave of business practice."

—Anjali Kumar, former head of Social Innovation at Warby Parker, former senior legal counsel for Google, and author of *Stalking God*

"A delightfully honest and insightful account of a mission-driven business and the diverse, sometimes funny, sometimes tortuous trajectory of that venture. His triumphs and mistakes, accompanied by dogged perseverance, make this not only a worthy read but valuable to any entrepreneur who is willing to get right up to their neck in something worth doing right."

—Chris Kilham, founder of Medicine Hunter, Inc.

"A beautiful book about how Amazonian plants can teach us to shapeshift our world—a powerful and illuminating message!"

—John Perkins, *New York Times* bestselling author of *Confessions of an Economic Hit Man*

"The case study of how Tyler and the Runa team innovate upon indigenous knowledge and translate it to benefit a diversity of stakeholders has great educational value."

—Dr. Florencia Montagnini, professor, Yale University

FULLY ALIVE

Using the Lessons of the Amazon to Live Your Mission in Business and Life

TYLER GAGE

ATRIA PAPERBACK

New York London Toronto Sydney New Delhi

An Imprint of Simon & Schuster, Inc.
1230 Avenue of the Americas
New York, NY 10020

First Atria Paperback edition August 2018

ATRIA PAPERBACK and colophon are trademarks of Simon & Schuster, Inc.

For information about special discounts for bulk purchases, please contact Simon & Schuster Special Sales at 1-866-506-1949 or business@simonandschuster.com.

The Simon & Schuster Speakers Bureau can bring authors to your live event. For more information, or to book an event, contact the Simon & Schuster Speakers Bureau at 1-866-248-3049 or visit our website at www.simonspeakers.com.

Interior design by Kyoko Watanabe

Manufactured in the United States of America

10 9 8 7 6 5 4 3 2 1

Library of Congress Cataloging-in-Publication Data

Names: Gage, Tyler, author.
Title: Fully alive : using the lessons of the Amazon to live your mission in business and life / Tyler Gage.
Description: First Edition. | New York : Atria Books, 2017.
Identifiers: LCCN 2017008696 (print) | LCCN 2017030936 (ebook) | ISBN 9781501156045 (eBook) | ISBN 9781501156021 (hardback)
Subjects: LCSH: Gage, Tyler. | Businessmen—Ecuador—Biography. | New business enterprises—Ecuador. | Success in business. | BISAC: BUSINESS & ECONOMICS / Motivational. | BUSINESS & ECONOMICS / Entrepreneurship. | BUSINESS & ECONOMICS / Development / Sustainable Development.
Classification: LCC HC201.5.G34 (ebook) | LCC HC201.5.G34 G34 2017 (print) | DDC 650.1—dc23
LC record available at https://lccn.loc.gov/2017008696

ISBN 978-1-5011-5602-1
ISBN 978-1-5011-5603-8 (pbk)
ISBN 978-1-5011-5604-5 (ebook)

To the guayusa leaf, for your spirited energy and your vital teachings

CONTENTS

CONTENTS

FULLY ALIVE

Introduction

Navigating Chaos

The subway rattled and shook as it jostled its way up to Midtown Manhattan. Listening to my headphones with my back straight and my hands folded neatly in my lap, I tried to focus on a recorded meditation. A man's soothing voice told me to "follow the sensations at the tip of your nose." I couldn't take it anymore and pulled the plug on my attempt to calm myself. Yanking my BlackBerry out of my pocket (yes, I still used a BlackBerry in 2015), I slouched forward in a ball of anger and changed tracks from the guided meditation to "I Don't Fuck with You" by Big Sean. The unambiguous refrain "*I don't give a fuck about you or anything that you do*" felt more in line with how I was feeling at the moment.

I couldn't believe what was happening. I was heading to a meeting with my board of directors, where I saw no other possible outcome than quitting or getting fired from my position as CEO of Runa, the company I had cofounded and nurtured like a baby. Only six years earlier I'd graduated from college, flown to Ecuador the next week, and sought to build a supply chain for guayusa, a revered Amazonian tea leaf that had never been commercially produced. (Forgive me for the early side note and cheesy phonetics, but it's pronounced "gwhy-you-sa" like "Gwhy-you-sa happy?")

My friend Dan MacCombie and I began by venturing into the Amazon with little more than our backpacks and our hearts full of terrified curiosity. Over the next few years we managed to build partnerships with thousands of indigenous farming families to sustainably produce guayusa, translating their rich traditions of relating to this plant into our core business model. Together we set out with a vision for the future of trade in the Amazon based on respectful exchange and healing, not exploitation and greed.

We then founded Runa and used this energizing leaf to make and sell organic iced teas and healthy energy drinks "from a leaf, not a lab," as we like to say. After years of hustle we'd become one of the fastest-growing beverage companies in the U.S., with millions of dollars in annual sales. We'd been featured on ABC's *Nightline*, raved about by Richard Branson, attracted major investors, and, most importantly, generated millions of dollars for the indigenous communities in Ecuador.

And here it was all about to end in some high-rise office building? Would all the sleepless nights, parasite infections, and deep prayers be rendered worthless by this horrid conclusion?

The meeting did not start well and only escalated for thirty minutes, with different members of the board taking their turns telling me how disappointed they were in me and how I was unfit to be a CEO. They said I wasn't listening, was being impatient, had failed to communicate like an adult—not to mention a good leader. Finally, one of them stood up, pounded the conference table, and screamed, "I could punch you in the face, you pompous child!"

And people think the tea business is all peace and love. Unable to express how devastated I was in the moment, I arrogantly chuckled at him and said, "Namaste to you too, you dick."

I had read that President Obama maintained a longstanding joke with his former advisor and friend Rahm Emanuel that speaks perfectly to the state of mind I found myself in at this moment. In a moment of defeat, the duo once imagined moving to Hawaii to open a T-shirt shack that sold only one size (medium) and one color (white). Their dream was that they would no longer have to make decisions. During difficult White House meetings when no good choices seemed possible, Mr. Emanuel would sometimes turn to Mr. Obama and say, "White." Mr. Obama would in turn say, "Medium."

Since medium white T-shirts can't be the answer, what do we do when things just don't seem to make sense; when we need to make a decision but our analysis could justify either course; or when our emotions and expectations blur our ability to see clearly? In this moment of complete breakdown with my board, my demons told me to throw in the towel, clock the guy, and piss it all away. But deeper down I knew that I couldn't choose the "I don't give a fuck" path, as much as I wanted to. Instead, I had to figure out how to navigate through the darkness.

This fundamental challenge is what drove me as an anxious, depressed teenager to the Amazon in the first place. I went looking for answers. Instead I found myself swallowed and digested by the weird world of shamanism and then spit back up into the equally strange world of entrepreneurship. The answers I found in these unexpected places weren't the easy or obvious ones. They often left me feeling more confused and lost than when I started. They forced me to endure before greater strength and guidance would be revealed.

I'm sure shamanism and entrepreneurship, let alone the intersection of the two, will at first strike most readers as completely irrelevant to their everyday realities. My goal in this book, however, is to reveal powerful tools and lessons from both of these worlds that can teach all of us how to grow toward and beyond our personal edges, no matter our circumstances. Stay with me here.

Shamanism and entrepreneurship are two disciplines that, at their core, teach and train you how to survive and thrive at the edges—of what you think is possible, of your comfort zone, of your sense of self. In learning how to have "both feet in both worlds," as I like to say, I've gained the courage, vision, and compassion to navigate the endless trials of building a business. Even more, this journey has helped me with the greater challenge of struggling to find and act with basic human goodness on a daily basis. Most days I succeed; some days I call someone a dick in a board meeting.

In the years I've spent in the Amazon, I've learned teachings and practices for personal and spiritual growth that are not only powerful in their own context but surprisingly translatable to the modern world. I've discovered an inherent pragmatism in these traditions that springs from a need to survive and a desire to thrive in one of the world's most lethal ecosystems: the

Amazon rainforest. These techniques were originally developed thousands of years ago for medicine and hunting, two of the most essential human needs. How we meet these needs has changed, but the basic underlying questions remain: How can I be healthier? How can I best accomplish my goals in a chaotic, uncertain world around me?

As someone with a strong repulsion to forced dogma and faith in detached beliefs, my desire for personal discovery grounded in direct experiences fit perfectly with the orientation of these shamanic practices. The Amazonian Kichwa people say that wisdom comes into the body through the feet, not from the head. They recognize that it's the path you walk in the world that creates insight and value, not the ideas you have in your mind. Rediscovering and applying the practices that forgotten peoples have used to traverse this fundamental puzzle of what it means to be human is one way to find strength through the trying times we find ourselves in.

The structure of the book follows my own story from growing up as a suburban kid to Amazonian misadventures to beverage industry warfare. I promise this is not a "Rah-rah, look at how great we are" tale. I'll share the things I think we've done right while building Runa, but I will spend more time being totally forthright about the intense struggles, personal crises, and many mistakes we've made along the way—and the steps we've taken to correct course. The mistakes are where the lessons are.

This book is not titled *Fully Alive* because I believe that at age thirty-one I have all the answers, nor do I subscribe to this idea that being fully alive is about being radiant, happy, and spiritually inspiring people all the time. In the indigenous Kichwa language, the deepest meaning of the word *runa* translates as "fully alive," meaning anything—plant, animal, or human—that is *willing* to embrace the fullness of life around them can rightfully be alive. Only in this way can we have true power and a connection to the animating forces of life in all their glory.

In this view, being fully alive comes from the union of extremes, and the excruciating, magnificent journey that weaves them together. To be able to truly feel joy, we must be willing to sit with grief. To know the lightness of the spirit, we must be open to the teachings of the shadow. To have the power to create, we must speak the language of logic and also the language of intuition. To completely appreciate Big Sean, we also need to follow the tingling at the tips of our noses. To find real understanding, we must get called a "pompous child" and see past the judgment to the underlying truth of the message being delivered. (Not only did I come to see that this comment was largely accurate, but this painful process with the board gave way to a necessary rebirth of the company. It felt classically shamanic, in that things had to get to their worst before there could be a purging and catharsis. But we will get to all that.)

Although it sounds trite to say it, it's absolutely true: the stars are brightest when the sky is darkest, and with the help of every brightly patterned puncture in our world of uncertainty we can navigate forward. This book is the story of one person's twists, turns, blocks, and breakthroughs toward that striving. I hope it challenges, inspires, and spurs you forward along your own path.

Chapter 1

Competing with Anxiety

My story definitely does not begin with shamans, poison dart frogs, or pristine rainforests—more like math teachers, miniature dachshunds, and suburban streets.

Some of my favorite days as a kid were spent with my grandfather, Clark Kerr, working in his garden, helping him harvest apples, prune old rosebushes, and trim daffodils. Then in his eighties, his slightly stooped posture and bald head made him look, at least to me, a bit like a lovable turtle. In the 1940s he and my grandmother had bought seven acres in the hills of El Cerrito, California, just north of Berkeley, for a total of $13,000. From the yard we could look out over the San Francisco Bay and take in a picturesque view of the Golden Gate Bridge.

My favorite part of my grandparents' home was the wall of artifacts in the dining room, filled with dozens and dozens of rare items and trinkets they had collected on their world travels from the 1930s through the 1980s: everything from Australian boomerangs to African masks. I loved to stand and study them, wondering just how all these strange mementos came to be on the wall, and if I would ever get to do cool things like they had done. At family dinners my grandparents kept me spellbound with stories about their adventures—from visiting Italy in the 1930s and being caught in a rally for Mussolini to hunting with pygmies in Africa. As children, my mom and two uncles joined them for many of their trips and always added their own twists to the endless stories.

My grandfather had grown up a Quaker on a small farm in Pennsylvania, and, keeping to his humble upbringing, was an extremely modest man. As a young kid, I didn't realize that it was special when we drove by the nearby University of California at Berkeley and my mom would point to "Grandpa's campus," or that it was unusual that framed copies of old *Time* magazines hung in the hallway of their house with his picture on the cover.

He'd been chancellor of UC Berkeley in the 1950s, and in 1958 was named president of the entire University of California system. During that time he designed the blueprint for public higher education in California with the vision that all Californians should have the opportunity to go to college for little to no cost. The network of community colleges, state schools, and University of California campuses was revolutionary back then and remains one of the leading public higher education systems in the world.

In the mid-1960s, protests for civil rights and against American involvement in the Vietnam War broke out on campuses all around the country, with Berkeley being especially charged. Conservative politicians in the state, led by a rising star named Ronald Reagan, demanded a police crackdown. In contrast, my grandfather believed in respecting others' opinions and hearing all sides of an argument, so he tried to keep order while giving the students the space to speak their minds.

In 1966, Reagan ran for governor and promised he would "clean up the mess" at Berkeley. After he won the election, Reagan pushed the UC board of regents to fire my grandfather, which it did. My mom laughs when she recounts that, from that moment on, he always muted the television when Ronald Reagan came on. Later in life he seldom spoke of his dismissal, but when he did, he joked that he left office the same way he had entered: "Fired with enthusiasm." I think about the way my grandfather showed up in his personal and professional life nearly every day, and at Runa have tried to live up to his example of creating dialogue and listening intently to all sides. I'm not nearly as even-tempered as he was, but I feel this same innate desire to hold space for multiple perspectives and try to live up to the model of respectful leadership he set.

My grandfather's understated aura was balanced by the fiery passion of my grandmother, Kay Kerr, who in 1961 cofounded Save the Bay, one of the first nonprofits in the early days of the environmental movement. It has played a huge role in establishing environmental protections for the San Francisco Bay and helped to open large sections of the shoreline for trails and parks. My grandmother was smart, opinionated, and generous, but also completely tenacious when it came to fighting for a cause she believed in; my own uncle even called her a "bulldog." She remained totally committed to her environmental work up to her death in 2010 at the age of ninety-nine. She certainly planted the seeds of environmental activism in me, and I'm sure some people might also accuse me of similar "bulldog" tendencies, based on the belief that there is always an intelligent solution to every problem that is worth fighting for.

My mom inherited her parents' caring spirit, love of nature, and passion for world travel, leading our family on exhausting vacations when my older sister, Lindsay, and I were kids. She once marked out all the ancient sites in Rome on a map and then marched us miles through the city through stifling 102-degree heat to make sure we didn't miss anything. Another time she made sure we got a "real" sense of Scotland by having us participate in sheep-shearing competitions and bagpipe festivals. Her love for understanding other cultures and amazement at the diversity of life was infectious to us kids.

My dad balanced out their relationship with hardcore hustle. As the son of a World War II veteran and a schoolteacher, he'd grown up relatively poor in the Glendale neighborhood of Los Angeles. After college he worked for Prudential until I was eight, when he quit to take a long shot and go out on his own as a commercial real estate broker. His charm, quick mind, and unbelievable work ethic allowed him to build a successful practice in Silicon Valley. When I was growing up, my dad was also a bit of a clown—literally. His hobby was riding unicycles, juggling, cracking eggs on his head—you know, the usual clown stuff. He taught me to ride his eight-foot-high unicycle, which he called "Gerry the Giraffe," when I was too young for Mom to be in even mild agreement.

But even with the incredible good fortune of being surrounded by this loving family and enjoying plenty of material comforts, I always suffered from some level of persistent anxiety. Beginning around the age of ten, I would often lie in bed and think about death—more specifically, the fact that one day I simply wouldn't be around anymore. Would I really just disappear? What would that be like? As the thought looped and looped in my brain, panic would finally set in and I'd end up sprinting for my parents' room, where I was comforted by hugs, murmurs, and a warm bed. These contemplations left me increasingly anxious deeper down. As I continued to develop, I felt more and more perplexed as to why no one *ever* talked about what seemed to me like a major elephant in the room—*the* elephant in the room—that doesn't conveniently go away, ever . . .

Either as a counterbalance or perhaps to distract myself from my own mind, I developed a distinct competitiveness and a tendency to hyper-focus. This asserted itself very early, sometimes in peculiar ways. For example, in first grade I decided I wanted to always be the first one to arrive to school. The gate at my elementary school opened at 7:00 a.m. so I started to wake up at 5:00 a.m. in order to get there an hour early and stake my place at the front of the line. As it happened, I had a nemesis, Robbie Schroeder, who had the same idea, so every morning was a contest.

This competitive drive found another, maybe more "normal" outlet: in youth soccer. I played on a select team coached by an intense former professional player from the Sudan, Mohamed Mohamed Mohamed (we called him "Mo"), who recruited players from across the Bay Area; my teammates included kids whose families were Mexican, Native American, Taiwanese, Brazilian, Austrian, Portuguese, Peruvian, Italian, and everything in between. We became a very good team and the closest of friends, giving me a sense of identity to help escape the sometimes isolating existential questions that continued to take on a life of their own in my head.

I was also an enthusiastic Boy Scout, eventually becoming an Eagle Scout. When I was sixteen I went on a three-week backpacking trip in northern New Mexico with other Scouts from around the country. It was physical, rugged, exhausting, and I loved it. Some days we hiked eighteen hours straight, from 6:00 a.m. to midnight, carrying all our gear, trudging up hills, and fording rivers. I loved the simplicity of waking up, cooking breakfast, and figuring out where we were going for the day. It felt raw and real.

One part of the trip was a "solo," which meant spending a day and a night alone in the woods with no food. During those twenty-four hours I *felt* the majesty of nature in a way I had never slowed down enough to really take in. The sense of inner peace and lightness I felt waking up by myself in the woods and having survived the night seemed to hit a level deeper than my anxious thoughts could reach, although I'm not sure I could have articulated that at the time.

While Quaker values were woven into my family's unspoken principles, overt spirituality or religion was totally absent. We never went to Quaker meetings and never talked about God or the afterlife at the dinner table, or ever. That time in the New Mexico wilderness by myself was the first spark I felt of *knowing*, somehow or some way, that there was more under the surface of life than I had imagined.

Thinking Body, Dancing Mind

Going into my junior year in high school, I was a decent soccer player—good enough to start on the team, but nowhere near great. Given my drive to win, this really frustrated me.

My mom had gone to a local sports medicine doctor named Michael Ripley for therapy. When she found out he was also a high-level performance coach who had trained, among others, many members of the U.S. Olympic sprint team, she suggested that I go see if he could help me with soccer.

When I showed up at his place I nearly left immediately after walking in the door. "Rip" lived by himself in a tiny house off a main street in the quaint suburban town of Orinda, where my family had moved. He was an intense curmudgeon who blasted hard-core rap from cassette tapes in his combination living room–gym, which reeked of cigar smoke. A former professional skydiver, he was a stocky five-foot-eight white guy, around sixty years old, with a head of white hair. Much as I later observed when working with shamans, you often find some of the greatest teachers in far-from-ostentatious circumstances that seem at odds with their immense skills.

His totally unconventional training techniques were based on doing a lot of high reps with low weights. He would, for example, have me do 180 step-ups onto a box with only 30 pounds of weights racked on a barbell. Every movement, however, had to be completely precise or his usual mumbling would become perfectly audible. "Practice makes perfect, huh?" he would puff. "Bullshit motherfucker. PERFECT practice makes perfect!"

His grueling physical exercises definitely made me faster, but what fascinated me most happened at the end of our training sessions, when Rip did a type of active-release massage therapy on my muscles. As I tried to block out the excruciating pain, he engaged my mind.

"Just imagine," he said one time as he dug into my hamstring, "a player on the other team has the ball. You see him across the field and know you need to get to him. You take off running, and as you go, you feel so light on your feet, every step natural and easy, your toes barely touching the ground. You close in on him with every stride, until you see the ball coming into reach. You slide and kick it away effortlessly."

In my next game, it felt eerie when the exact scenario he described happened: I ran across the field faster than I ever had and slide-tackled a player with the ball. It felt like I had suddenly been powered up to a new level of playing ability, at least as much through the visualization exercises as the physical training. It was so new, strange, and powerful that I sort of felt like I was on mental steroids. What the hell was going on?

The next day I told Rip what happened and asked him to explain more about *how* the visualization stuff worked and *why* it worked.

After a bit of his usual grumbling, he grabbed a book off the shelf above his desk. It was *Thinking Body, Dancing Mind*, a guide to improving sports and business performance by Chungliang Al Huang, a Taoist monk, and Jerry Lynch, a coach.

I took it home and devoured it. The approach to sports it prescribed was the opposite of the stressful system in which I'd grown up. Most coaches push their players to perform and reinforce their expectations through punishment: if you fail to get the rebound or hit the crossing pass, they yell at you or bench you.

In contrast, the book's Taoist approach urges us to be joyful in our activities, to take pleasure in the expression of our talents, and to simply be in the moment. We derive strength from being in tune with the world around us, not pushing against it and imposing our own arbitrary goals. The irony is that, by doing this, our performance actually *increases* and we end up doing even better than we imagined.

The book includes guided sets of meditations and affirmations, which I diligently worked through before going to bed and before games. This method led to such an incredible improvement in my abilities that in my senior year, while playing center defender, I was one of the leading scorers in Northern California.

I was stunned. Up until that point in my life, I'd thought you were basically born with a set of talents and were pretty much stuck. Since I was a decent but not exceptional athlete, my soccer skills would then be limited to those physical talents. But by accessing different layers of my mind, I exceeded all expectations I'd had for my own performance. It's something I saw much later as an entrepreneur when founding Runa: more often than not, we define our own limitations in our heads. By breaking out of our common mental ruts, we can perform at levels that we would have once thought impossible.

All of this was like discovering a vast new continent to explore, one in which I had only taken the first tentative step. It fed my growing suspicion that there was a lot going on in life that for some reason was just slightly obscured from us. That in turn fueled my anxiety and depression. It felt like the more I glimpsed moments of connection with nature and experienced deeper layers of my mind, the more friction, weight, and general dissatisfaction I felt in my "normal" life. Thirsty to learn more, I ramped up my literary adventures to include existential philosophy, evolutionary biology, and whatever else that seemed to offer an entry into these hidden worlds.

In a bookstore on Telegraph Avenue in Berkeley, I stumbled upon *Exploring the World of Lucid Dreams*, a book based on the research of Stanford professor Stephen LaBerge. It introduced me to lucid dreaming: when you realize you're dreaming while you're in a dream and learn to control what happens. A lucid dreamer can travel to different worlds, work on solving problems, address family and emotional issues, and confront and resolve nightmares. It was this last aspect that appealed to me most as my high levels of existential anxiety were leading to terrifying nightmares.

In addition to detailing the results of Dr. LaBerge's studies, the book also laid out a series of simple steps to start lucid dreaming. I began practicing a "reality test" exercise, where you constantly ask yourself if you are dreaming or awake during your daily life, which in turn leads you to ask the same question when you're actually asleep. Within a few days I started lucid dreaming. The exercises were so simple and effective, it seemed laughable. But the experience was exhilarating, like I'd gotten some mental Mario Bros. mushroom boost, being able to fly, make things disappear, and do other things . . . (Yes, I *was* a teenage boy.)

On a few occasions I was able to interact with my nightmares and find ways to remove myself from stressful dream scenarios of being chased by gangsters or held hostage, waking up refreshed and more confident instead of exhausted and anxious.

Why wasn't anyone talking about these tools for personal

empowerment? Why was *I* the weird one for using visualization to be a better soccer player and using lucid dreaming to help reduce my stress? Despite the many comforts and support I was given by my family and surroundings, I felt confused and disappointed on a deeper level, wondering what this game of life we are all playing is really about. I sensed that whole layers of experience were being completely ignored in my suburban cocoon.

My seemingly miraculous athletic development led to a totally unexpected offer to play soccer at Brown University. I hadn't even been considering the school, but since it was a highly ranked Division 1 team, I was definitely in. On top of that, Brown had a reputation as being a pretty eccentric place, so that struck me as even better.

My transition was not nearly as smooth as I had hoped. Although I played in almost every game and started in most during my freshman year, the overly macho culture of the soccer team grated on me, as it was far from the brotherhood I'd felt with my team growing up.

At the same time my interest in nature reawakened, thanks in large part to a class I took at the start of my freshman year called Religion Gone Wild: Spirituality and the Environment. Admittedly, by the title alone, it did little to counter the stereotype of Brown as a hippie paradise. The purpose of the course was to explore the ways that various indigenous peoples, Buddhists, and poets around the world view the fundamental relationship between the human spirit and the natural world.

Entering Brown, I had planned to study environmental public policy: inspired by both of my grandparents, I thought that working within large institutions such as the government or a big international NGO would be the best way to change our disastrous environmental policies. Religion Gone Wild offered a much more personal take on the often abstracted idea of what we normally refer to as "the environment." Our reading list included the work of farmer and writer Wendell Berry, Zen monks, and "On the Importance of Owning Chickens," an essay written by our professor, Mark S. Cladis, that really touched me. In it Professor Cladis writes about how owning and tending to the needs of three hens helped him intimately see that he is not at the center of nature but part of it. Even though he cares for the chickens, he has no control over them: they live out their dharma just as he lives out his.

The core of the essay asks: Do we, as humans, relate to the world around us as rulers or in wonderment at our roles in a system that works beyond any of our attempts to control it? "Some claim we inhabit a world increasingly dominated by an instrumental reason that imprisons us by a vast system of calculated, rationalized labor," Cladis writes. "Perhaps. A latch is within reach, however. A way of escape. It may not land us in the promised land, but it does lead to a more promising place. We have some say. We can turn off the television, renounce hectic amusements, and discover the re-creation of good work: working well, working with care and patience, working toward excellence and joy."

The attentiveness, vulnerability, and gentleness of the essay made me tear up as I read it in the back row of a hard-hitting political science class that I was quickly losing interest in. I'd felt these sentiments while backpacking in high school but had been unable to articulate or understand them.

I didn't see how anything we were learning in class could have any practical use in the "real" world, but the confused ten-year-old inside of me appreciated at least being part of conversations about what it means to exist and what exists beneath the surface of things.

In other ways I felt like I was walking on a path of loose dirt on the side of a mountain with a steep fall should I slip. Even though I'd achieved the singular goal I'd been pushed toward since I was a kid—getting into a good college—I felt fundamentally out of place and unsure of myself. That helped to amplify my long-term, recurring anxiety into more full-on depression. I began smoking more weed, in part to reinforce the "cool-kid" California identity I was going for, but underneath I was just trying to ease the confusion and emptiness I felt in this new place for which I'd had such high hopes. The day after the soccer season ended, I remember eating so many ganja brownies that I blacked out and woke up twenty-four hours later on the floor of my room. I just wanted to shut off the feelings and shut out the world around me that was failing to answer the questions I didn't even know how to ask.

As often happens in life and business, everything inside me was screaming for change; I just needed to quiet down and listen to the message.

As I was trying to find my way forward, I read about Mark Allen, a six-time winner of the Hawaii Ironman Triathlon in the late 1980s and early 1990s. (To clarify, an Ironman is a 3-mile swim in the open ocean, then a 100-mile bike ride, topped off by running a full 26.2-mile marathon.)

Before his massive success in the race, Mark had finished six times in the top five but had never won. He credited his breakthrough to working with a shaman from Mexico's Huichol tribe. He said the shamanic approach had completely shifted his perspective, teaching him to trust in life, to feel gratitude for where he was, and to believe that even if things weren't going to be easy, they were going to work out if he let go of his need for control. He called his immersion in shamanism the "final key" that put him over the top.

"Most athletes use their physical being to win," he wrote in the article. "Some train their emotions. Very few here in the Western world train their spirit. And without a doubt this is one of the most overlooked ways for performance to be improved."

While I was curious about shamanism from my readings, the image in my head was that of a guy in some fancy traditional costume banging a drum and waving around some feathers. How in the world could this help an elite athlete win one of the world's most grueling contests? Winning the Ironman six times was certainly not some supernatural mumbo jumbo.

I reached out to Mark directly, who asked if I wanted to take part in a retreat he was helping to lead that summer in California at Mount Shasta with Brant Secunda, his longtime shaman. Count me in! I said. About forty people came. We camped at the base of the mountain, amid pine trees and next to a clear river. Mark was a very humble, down-to-earth, straightforward guy.

One of the first activities was a sweat lodge ritual. They erected a large dome out of willow branches and canvas tarps. Each step of the ceremony was intentional, every relationship named and recognized. A raging fire was built outside to heat a pile of volcanic rocks into large glowing eggs that would serve as the centerpiece of the lodge. We honored each rock as it was brought in, thanking it for the heat it provided and for helping us purify. As the heat rose in the lodge, we sang traditional songs. As an introverted athlete, singing wasn't high on my list of favorite activities, but when you feel like your skin is about to burn off, singing your heart out becomes a pretty awesome thing to do.

Finally we were let out. Trying not to seem too desperate, I briskly walked-ran to the river and plunged in, reveling as the cold water touched my skin, completely refreshed. The birds' chirping sounded clearer, the light reflecting on the pine trees looked crisper, and I felt the pulsing of my heartbeat like never before. It was amazing how this ritual brought me back into my body and awakened a visceral connection with the natural world.

Brant had a family-friendly teaching style, and his spiritual jokes were corny but spot-on. "Make believe you're happy and you might just trick yourself," he would say with a sly smile. We told our dreams around the fire every morning before Brant gave teachings about Huichol traditions, the universe, and God.

Brant told us the Huichol people believe that humans contain deep spiritual wisdom within themselves but that we have mostly forgotten it. Because of this, the most important prayer they have in the Huichol tradition is the prayer for *memory*—not progress, not achievement, and not advancement, but memory.

They believe that if we constantly remind ourselves of the deeper currents of life that support our every passing breath, that we too can be carried in the simple flow of life, of family, and of honoring that which has come before us and will prevail long after. These practices of acknowledgment speak directly to this prayer for memory. Rather than trying to create or make something new, they recognize that often it's much harder to simply see what's actually present, just as it is. Our job is to clear away the layers of confusion and doubt that only make life *seem* hard and complicated so that we can remember how glorious it really is.

I intermittently felt touched and troubled by the radical simplicity of this perspective. My mind went to work poking holes in Brant's philosophy. Still, I couldn't dismiss the *feeling* around it. When I just breathed and absorbed the teachings and beauty around me, I was enveloped with awe. I was finding that the more I let go and allowed myself to be "lost," the better I felt.

The last part of the retreat was a vision quest, which was a day and a night alone in the forest without food or water, similar to what I had done as an Eagle Scout in high school. I walked out of the camp and hiked up until I found a ridge with a view of Mount Shasta, where I acknowledged the pine trees around me, the birds, the insects, and the four directions, and established myself among them.

The first thing you realize when you can't eat or drink is the incredible amount of stuff we shovel into our mouths every day without thinking about it. The second is that you don't really know how slowly time can pass. You experience everything in pull-your-hair-out slow motion, from each minuscule change in the color of the sky at sunset to every stage of physical sensation that occurs when an ant bites the outside of your left ankle. You are pulled into the present moment whether you like it or not, and as time passes, you find yourself more vulnerable to your thoughts and emotions as well.

With nothing to distract me, I felt the full force of the unhappiness I'd experienced my freshman year at Brown and my crushing uncertainty about what to do with my life. I felt like each of my limbs had been tied to different horses running in opposite directions, and the pressure of it all was going to tear me apart. As I lay down on my tarp that night I wished there was something that I could have studied that would have better prepared me for this—some knowledge that could give me perfect clarity and banish all my doubts. If only I could lasso the thick, tightly wound rope of my mind around my uncertainty and cage it up—or, if it put up too much of a fight, strangle it into submission.

This desire for *control*, which I've often felt as CEO of a company, relentlessly clashed with the feeling underneath that there was something trying to be born. It was hard to be vulnerable and to admit that I didn't have all the answers; in fact, I felt confused and lost. When we look back, it's always nice to pinpoint these turning points and tell a nice story around them; but it's easy to forget the fear and terror and that, as it happens, you feel like you're getting emotionally beaten up by Mike Tyson in his prime.

My stomach churned at the thought of going back to Brown, but the "rational" part of me insisted it would be crazy to leave a prestigious school. Yet, being out there with none of my usual distractions, I heard every fiber of my being screaming, *Something has to change!*

Chapter 2

Clear Your Filters

Needless to say, my parents weren't exactly thrilled when I came home from the Huichol retreat and told them I was going to drop out of Brown. Instead of trying to argue with me, which they had long ago learned was usually futile, they took their standard approach of letting me fall on my face on my own accord. They simply suggested I take a leave of absence instead of quitting entirely.

While I considered my next move, I enrolled in a few organic agriculture and mythology courses at UC Santa Cruz and took a hypnotherapy course in an attempt to find alternate techniques to deal with my anxiety.

The story I had about needing to understand, needing to control whatever was below the surface, seemed more and more like a story that was writing me, rather than the other way around.

There was some intangible feeling beneath it that I knew I had to get to but wasn't sure how, and I was now feeling my way through the dark toward what I hoped would be an answer.

Poking around online late one night, I read about Joe, an ethnobotanist who had worked with indigenous tribes in South America for nearly two decades and seemed to have an encyclopedic knowledge of Amazonian plants and their medical uses. Characteristic of the mundane ways I was venturing into deeper levels of weirdness, I googled him and sent him an email. We often think something "magical" needs to happen out of the blue for it to be "properly spiritual," but I've found it often starts with something as simple as a few clicks on the keyboard. He wrote back that he was coming to Berkeley the next week and would be happy to meet.

Hyperintelligent and fiery, Joe captivated me with his tales from the jungle. He told me he had many years of journals stacked up and wanted to write a book about Amazonian plants. To my surprise, he invited me to be his assistant. After finishing my finals three weeks later, I joined him at the eco-lodge and yoga retreat center he had started on the Pacific coast of Costa Rica.

Arriving at the retreat center was like stepping into the Garden of Eden. The lodge was right at the edge of the rainforest, a collection of bungalows just steps from a secluded white-sand beach. Capuchin monkeys played in the trees, and scarlet macaws squawked from their perches nearby. You could not have designed a more idyllic tropical environment.

Every morning Joe woke me at four to take advantage of what he saw as a "creative portal" that opened around sunrise, and then told free-form, highly circuitous stories about his work in South America as I frantically took notes. His dedication to the cause as well as his anger at some of the tragedies he'd seen was truly moving. He would tear up while telling stories of indigenous elders being murdered and thousands of acres of land getting stolen from different communities.

To get us going, Joe brewed strong pots of tea from the leaves of a bushy shrub growing near his house. He told me he'd brought the plant up from Ecuador, where the indigenous people swore by its power to help overcome their fears, get guidance from their dreams, and deepen their connection to the natural world.

I wasn't sure what any of that meant exactly, but I loved the delicious, slightly sweet taste and the unusual caffeine buzz the tea imparted—almost like it provided energy that lifted you up from the inside out, rather than slapping you in the face and prying open your eyes like an energy drink or a triple espresso might.

The tea in question was none other than guayusa, the plant that would become the inspiration and staple of my future organization, Runa. I sometimes wish I had a more captivating story about my first experience drinking this leaf that would eventually turn my life upside down—some brilliant "Aha!" moment when I immediately knew it was something special and that I would devote years of my life to this plant. But it didn't happen that way. Some guy woke me up at 4:00 a.m. and we drank some guayusa together. Simple as that.

For me personally, the story of my first encounter with guayusa is actually more inspiring for its simplicity. If everything in life was immediately clear and striking, there would be no need for any journey of discovery or any questioning. Did you experience something today or meet someone who might change your life in years or decades to come? From moment to moment, we have absolutely no idea, which makes each encounter all the more mysterious, humbling, and full of possibility. Even when we don't know exactly where we want to go, by heading in the direction of our curiosity, we plant seeds that may wondrously bloom years later.

Into the Amazon

During my time in Costa Rica, I read a book called *Secrets of the Shamans: Tapping the Spirit Power Within You* by Jose Stevens and his wife, Lena. Jose was a clinical psychologist from New Mexico who had studied with shamans for decades. His writing was both intelligent and heartfelt, and there was an approachability in his tone that attracted me. I wrote to him explaining my situation and that I wanted to learn more about this path. His response paralleled the one I had received from Mark Allen: he told me he was soon taking a small group to Peru to work with some Amazonian shamans and invited me to join. Given that Joe and I were not making much progress on his book, I decided it was time to move on.

I flew to Pucallpa, Peru, a port city of two hundred thousand people on the Ucayali River, one of the three major tributaries of the Amazon. Pucallpa, along with Iquitos, a bigger jungle city downriver, is something of a mecca for Amazonian shamanism in its many forms. It is also a transit point for shipping timber and other forest products out of the Amazon. I found it to be hot, dirty, and loud, one of the most awful places I've ever been. A generally seedy vibe permeated everything from the buzzing flocks of motor taxis to the stench of rotting fish wafting from market stalls.

I met Jose in a hotel restaurant, where he shared a table with his daughter and six other people he'd brought along. Everyone else was between forty-five and sixty-five. The group included a psychotherapist, a musician, a computer programmer, a stay-at-home mom, a real estate broker, and a nun (yes, a nun). Jose embodied a rare mixture of intelligence and sweetness, and I immediately felt comfortable under his guidance.

Jose told us that the territory surrounding Pucallpa was the heart of the traditional lands of the Shipibo, an indigenous tribe of some forty thousand people. He said their shamans were known for their exceptional knowledge of plants, and we were going to work with a few of them.

The next day we took a boat from the waterfront, speeding one and a half hours up the wide river, hawks circling over the shoreline. Our destination was Yarinacocha (meaning "Serpent Lake"—inviting, I know). A village of about two thousand people, it's the largest of more than two hundred Shipibo villages in the Ucayali river basin, and much closer to Pucallpa than the majority of Shipibo villages, which can be up to a nine-day boat ride away. On the banks of the lagoon, Jose's longtime friend and teacher Herlinda Augustín Flores awaited us.

She was small of stature but bursting with life, around fifty years old, with jet-black bangs hanging to her eyes and a Cheshire cat smile. She emanated a powerful joy that energized the air around her. In a more understated fashion, her husband Enrique shared her brightness and warmly greeted our posse of sweaty gringos. Their many children, cousins, nieces, and nephews flocked around, holding our hands, kicking soccer balls, and making fast friends.

The *Dieta*

We were in Yarinacocha for ten days to undergo a plant *dieta*, the entry point into the world of Amazonian plant medicine and a pillar of Amazonian shamanism similar in importance as meditation is to Buddhism. The *dieta* (which directly translates to "diet" but the connotations in English make it an inaccurate representation) is a precise methodology developed by shamans over thousands of years whereby you consume preparations of specific plants that are said to provide healing and empowerment on every level, from the body to the mind to the spirit.

Out of the fifty thousand–plus plants in the Amazon, there is a core set of a few hundred specific plants, often referred to as "master plants," that are consistently used across different tribes for apprenticeship and healing *dietas*. The shamans would say that plants in this particular class have a degree of healing ability that "normal" plants don't have: beyond just mending the physical body, they are said to somehow help repair the psycho-emotional wounds that are often the underlying source of physical illness. It's like they have deep taproots into the subconscious world, whereas other plants have shallow root systems, so to speak. However, these master plants are not at all "psychedelic" or "hallucinogenic," as one might immediately think "crazy Amazonian plants" might be.

To start our *dietas*, we had to restrict our usual consumption patterns, which meant cutting out sugar, salt, alcohol, pork, marijuana, oil, and sex, among many other things. "The dietary restrictions are sort of like doing a deep clean on your house before a distinguished guest comes over," Jose said.

Moreover, Herlinda stressed, "the plants speak quietly." In other words, we had to calm down and get away from the ups and downs of our everyday lives that override our access to subtler perceptions. From an indigenous point of view, going from salty chips, to spicy salsa, to sugary drink, to a horror movie, to a beer, to sex or masturbation, to Facebook, to yelling at your friend, to watching a Jimmy Fallon clip on YouTube, are the psycho-emotional equivalent of the jerks, loops, and queasiness of the steepest roller coaster at Six Flags.

I came to see that a principal intention of the *dieta* was to move us from a state of *ingestion* to *digestion*. Abstaining from the constant input overload of our daily lives freed up energy that could be directed toward processing lingering chunks of unresolved experiences, traumas, and patterns across our physical, mental, emotional, and spiritual selves.

Herlinda told our group that we would be dieting two plants that are considered sisters: *piñon blanco* and *piñon colorado*.

She told us the Shipibo regard *piñon blanco* as being deeply connected to divine light and use it to flush, clean, and purify. *Piñon colorado*, on the other hand, is used to more directly combat darkness, hostility, and negative intentions. Herlinda said that it can unravel old traumas and uncork emotional blocks. Dieting these plants was supposed to help us break through to deeper levels of our own awareness. In practical terms, that meant we all got up at the break of dawn, gathered outside, and chugged twelve-ounce cups of freshly juiced leaves from the two plants. Spicy, putrid grass clippings, anyone?

After that, we were given cigars made of *mapacho*, the local name for a certain type of jungle tobacco (botanical name *Nicotiana rustica*) that has twenty-five times the nicotine content of normal tobacco. Herlinda had us place the cigars on our hearts and think about our intentions for the day and what we wanted the plants to help with. Then we smoked the *mapachos* and blew tobacco smoke onto our own bodies and then up into the sky, taking the smoke only into our mouths. The Shipibo regard tobacco as a powerful tool for spiritual cleaning, guidance, and protection, but recognize its dangers. Jose said a Shipibo man once asked him, "So people in your country put the tobacco smoke into their lungs?" Jose confirmed that was the case. "That's crazy. That will kill you!" the man shrieked.

After consuming the plants, we walked a little way to a hut in the jungle, where we spent the day in silence, sleeping in hammocks, journaling, reading, and meditating, lulled by the humidity and bird chirps. From the first day I felt electrified, as if I was vibrating on a new level. (Again, the nicotine helped in that department I'm sure.)

My inner conflicts emerged poignantly and vividly. I saw the constant fight within myself, between the side of me that wanted to be a goodie-goodie who did well in school and made everyone happy, and the other, competing urge to rebel against everything, exhausted by the energy it took to be pleasant, respectable, and nonintrusive. One side feeling hollow and stressed, the other sad and angry.

The basic *dieta* restrictions essentially help you take off your shell, so to speak, and then drinking the master plants is like plugging your subconscious into an amplifier. It's as if the plant medicines somehow have direct access to all the shit that we keep *just* below the surface of our everyday existence—the painful stuff that may pop up in moments of vulnerability or stress, but for the most part we keep suppressed in order to function in our day-to-day lives. Most importantly, they also have the ability to dive another layer deeper, underneath the shit, to the raw life force and what might be called soul substance—sources of tremendous healing power and inspiration.

One day I went to sit by a tree a bit away from the hut. After closing my eyes, I began to doze off. I saw a perfectly clear vision of an intense goat wearing a jester hat and shiny hoop earrings and sticking its tongue out at me. *Strange,* I thought. Then the goat started to cry. I heard something crack in the middle of my chest like a joint popping, and all of a sudden I started to bawl uncontrollably. For a while I couldn't stop thinking, *This is ridiculous. Stop. Stop now. There is no* reason *to be crying. Nothing even* happened. *Come on man, get your shit together!*

But then, surprisingly, it started to feel good. I followed that feeling through many rounds of sniffling, snorting, sobbing, and hyperventilating before lying down and feeling the weight of my own body like never before. I felt lighter, more full in myself, and like I'd let something go, although I was utterly perplexed as to what that was.

Bizarre? Absolutely. Relevant? Can't say so—I have never owned a goat or worn hoop earrings. Useful? Absolutely. In retrospect, I can definitely make out the symbolism of the tough, eat-anything goat as a representation of my stubborn personality, and the jester hat as a mockery of my ego's futile attempts to disguise its hardened countenance.

For years I'd been trying to get past the surface of my mind, to find something beneath the ordinary layers of stress, anxiety, guilt, fear, and duty that afflict us all. Techniques such as the visualizations I'd used to get better at soccer, experiments with lucid dreaming and hypnosis, and most certainly the Huichol retreat at Mount Shasta had lit the way, but nothing seemed to help me fully break through.

I was exploring areas that somehow went beyond the rational mind, but I was desperately "trying to understand" all of it. It felt like such a noble and defensible task, right? Who doesn't want to try to understand things? Somehow this *dieta* helped me see that my need to understand was really about a desire to be in control, instead of just being present. I began to realize that my seemingly worthy need to understand was a trap: it was my anxiety in disguise. After my bout of crying in the jungle, I jotted down a simple distillation of this insight: *Trust the feeling, not the story.*

Letting It Go

During the *dieta,* every other night we would gather in one of the main huts to meditate and listen to the shamans sing. The shamans drank a plant brew they called *nishi* (known as ayahuasca in other traditions) that they said opened their vision to see and helped them understand the source of sickness or pain in each patient.

The rhythmic songs they chanted are called *bewe* in Shipibo (pronounced "buh-wuh," with the "wuh" being pronounced in a guttural staccato), hauntingly beautiful tunes with cascading melodies, often sung in a falsetto pitch. They sang dozens of *bewe* throughout the night, approaching six to eight hours of nonstop singing, often with three or four shamans crooning different *bewe* all at once—a polyphonic experience that could be alternatingly enchanting and highly irritating.

What fascinated me was that the *bewe* aren't songs as we know them: they have no defined structure and no set lyrics. Each shaman pulls from a wide range of ancient rhythms and melodies, and then improvises the words, which usually carry healing invocations and intentions. Jose related that "the Shipibo see humans as a singing species, like the birds, but many of us have forgotten how to sing. If someone gets sick, a shaman might ask them 'When did you stop singing?' "

The songs felt totally penetrating and healing at the deepest layers of my being. Sometimes one of the shamans would go around the room, sit in front of each person, and sing directly to each of us. One night I felt wretched and shaky during the ceremony, but when Herlinda came around to sing directly to me, it felt like she was shuffling the deck of my soul and playing solitaire with my mind. Afterward I felt inexplicably happier, lighter, and shinier. The effect was startling.

During the first few days of the *dieta* I developed a feeling of stillness and attention to inner detail that felt unencumbered and deeply receptive. At least some small or large part must have been due to the change in routine and the disruption of my normal patterns: being out in the jungle, giving up sugar and salt, being away from the Internet. But it felt like there was also an X factor at play, like the plants were penetrating into my bone marrow and breaking into my blood cells.

But as the days went on, things got more real. By day five I felt exhausted, depressed, angry, and super-hazy. Frustrated and covered in mosquito bites, I huffed over to Jose.

"The plants are making me feel even more depressed than I was before," I lamented.

He smiled. "Sounds like the plants might be bringing up things for you to look at. The plants don't really *make* you feel things, they help you see what's already there. Maybe there is something deeper they are pulling to the surface to help you let go of."

Seemingly out of nowhere, Herlinda appeared: "*Déjalo Tailor. 'Pija pija vainkin' como digamos nosotros.*" ("Just drop it, Tyler. 'Let it go, let it go all day' as we say.")

Jose added, "That's one of the trickiest things about the *dieta*. It puts you in a very vulnerable state of self-reflection and sensitivity: it can get pretty confusing in there, but letting go and trusting the process is the key. You can also ask the plants to help you see what might be going on under the surface."

"Take this cloth and put it over your body. It's a special song to help release ideas and feelings that no longer serve you," Herlinda said. She handed me a beautiful traditional black Shipibo textile and walked away.

Shipibo weavings feature stunning, intensely patterned geometric shapes woven in resplendent colors on large pieces of cloth. To the Shipibo, they are not just weavings but *songs*. They are the visual translation of the healing songs they sing, said to carry the same powerful vibrations to heal.

Going back to my hammock as the sun was setting, I collapsed into it facedown and wrapped the blanket around my shoulders and head. "*Piñon colorado* and *piñon blanco*, if you are listening, please help me let go. I don't want to hold on to these feelings anymore," I said to myself before scolding myself for having just tried to talk to these plants. Then I promptly passed out.

I found myself in a dream in a crowded, dirty old 1900s English train station, sitting at a desk piled with paperwork: receipts, memos, legal-looking documents with stamps and seals on them that I had to review and sign. People were piling onto a train on a nearby track and the whistle blew.

I knew that I had to get on that train before it left but needed to finish this paperwork first. Breathing fast, grabbing different sheets of nonsense, I frantically signed things and shuffled the stacks around. Becoming more and more confused and anxious, I stood up and yelled, "What the fuck! I don't even know what to do with this!"

And then I realized: *Because you don't need to do any of it . . .*

Oh . . . huh . . . I guess that's right, I thought, softly surprised.

The train whistled again. I strolled over to it, a bit bewildered, and climbed the steps. Entering the cabin, I turned left, and found myself in a tropical garden. The air went from musky and clogged to floral and dew filled. Hummingbirds zipped by. Incredible flowers I'd never seen before sprouted up everywhere in intricate geometric patterns.

Elated, I sort of dance-floated gleefully throughout the garden, then noticed a radiant being floating toward me. Wrapped in brightly colored fabrics, it appeared to be some kind of ethereal demigod. As it got closer, I noticed intricate golden jewelry around its neck and arms. Then I realized it was heading right at me; I froze as it came straight into my body. And then I jolted awake.

Short of breath, I glanced around, and started laughing so hard that I fell from my hammock, tears streaming from my eyes. *What the heck was* that? I wondered. I had no clue, but I felt immensely lighter and that somehow I had let something major go.

Pija is one of the most important words in Shipibo shamanic healing. It means to let go, to surrender, or to throw away. It's often used when a shaman is trying to expel some type of sickness from a person's body, but it more deeply reflects the spirit of letting go.

Later on, I saw that the experience of doing *dietas* helped me get comfortable with letting things go and avoid the trap of analyzing everything to death. As an entrepreneur, this has been of critical importance: things go wrong, plans don't work out, deals fall through, and you have to *let them go.* Of course there is a temptation to stew over your missteps and mistakes, but the best course is to glean the lessons and move on. When you hold on to something—old hurts, plans that didn't work out, outdated ideas—you are blocking the opportunity to receive fresh ideas and inspiration.

I can't say I "understood" most of what was happening during that first trip to Yarinacocha, but I felt like I was shedding old skin. But something about the experience hit a deeper chord with me: the enchanting *bewe* songs, the foul tasting plants, the illumination of the Yarinacocha lagoon in the morning light.

It struck me that the Shipibo had developed a structured approach to access deeper layers of our consciousness, repair inner wounding, and help us "*jiwe*." I loved this word, *jiwe*, which essentially means "to come back to life." I felt restored, replenished, repaired, and invited back into a fresh feeling of myself, an open sensitivity to the rising of the sun each day, and a heart more receptive to the laughter and joy of each moment. The brilliance of the Shipibo system was that it offered a way to clear the static in our lives and allow us to lock into the signal.

Rather than flooring the gas pedal, and even before turning on the car, the first step is to clean the windshield. This means taking a squeegee to the lens of our basic capacity *to see*, which shamans consider more than just looking at things. Unfortunately, this lens often gets scratched, smeared, and fogged up by our habitual patterns, buried traumas, and compulsive mental habits.

Over time I've had to find ways to clear my filters and gain spaciousness within my daily routine and workflow as well. Revitalizing my ability to both see clearly and be prepared for the unpredictability of life in each moment is critical, but doing shamanic plant *dietas* certainly isn't the only way to do it.

While the master plants and the *dieta* are the tools the Shipibo developed to blast the grime from our intuitive windshield, we all have tools available to us that can help clear our filters that don't require a trip to Peru. In my daily life, the single most useful tool I use is silent meditation. The practice of open breathing and focusing on the appearance of thoughts, rather than the thoughts themselves, is perfectly in harmony with the methodology of the *dieta*. It gives me a critical ability to not get caught up in my thoughts throughout the day.

Salt baths are another one of my go-tos, using high concentrations of Dead Sea salt, Epsom salt, and particular essential oils with clearing characteristics; cedar, frankincense, and lavender are some personal favorites. If that's not hippie enough for you, put on some Enya. In addition to the hot water being obviously relaxing and soothing, salt, from a shamanic perspective, is said to clear and dissolve subtle, unharmonized energies.

A final challenge, and one that I'm ever more dogged about in my own life, is not looking at my phone as soon as I wake up.

I've found that the shock of transitioning so bluntly from subconscious dream space to frenetic bubble messages in blue light seems to disorient me in such a fundamental way that it frays my ability to *see* the coming day and feel good in my body. Even twenty minutes of establishing myself in physical reality and feeling grateful to have another day to learn and breathe makes a world of difference. I still use my phone as my alarm clock, just on airplane mode. (I hear they still make alarm clocks, though.)

Bridging Worlds

I spent the next two and a half years of my life on a sort of walkabout, trying to learn about the language of the plants—almost a self-directed liberal arts course in shamanism. The backbone of that time was going back and forth to Yarinacocha to do *dietas* with Herlinda and her family. While she mostly became intent on convincing me to marry one of her daughters, she always welcomed me back and provided a safe space to learn from the plants.

During this time, I also returned to Brown, which drew me back when I realized that pursuing a literary arts degree would not only provide a platform to express what I learned in the Amazon but also require very little in terms of mandatory coursework. That meant I could do lots of independent studies that would allow me to stay in the Amazon, where I wanted to focus on translation and transcription of Amazonian songs, poetry, and myths.

In the summer before my senior year, I went back to Peru to do another *dieta* with Herlinda, who had a special tree extract she got for me from one of her teachers upriver. He brought it down and also performed a few nights of healing sessions on Herlinda, who had become quite sick with uterine cancer and was really struggling.

Herlinda's illness added both sadness and a sense of urgency to the *dieta*. As I spent more and more time in her village, I became increasingly aware of the overlap between the modern and indigenous worlds. One constant was the whine of chain saws in the jungle.

I remember confronting Pascal, one of Herlinda's sons, on a humid afternoon. The day before, he'd told me an incredible story about how the *chaikuni jonibo*, the legendary master Shipibo shamans, knew how to turn themselves into tree spirits and could live in the old hardwoods long after their physical bodies had passed. "That's why we do *dietas* with big trees and have to be respectful to them," he said.

Less than twenty-four hours later, he came back from cutting down an old mahogany tree with a group of men from the village. Their excited, giddy expressions about selling the wood for a chunk of change infuriated me.

"Pascal, how is it that you can sit there one day and tell me a story about how your ancestors live in the trees, and the next day you're ripping one down?" I asked, trying to control myself.

"If you had to choose between cutting down a tree or sending your child to school, what would you choose?" he asked me. "What if the choice was between keeping a tree standing or paying for Mom to go to the hospital?"

I could hear resignation in his voice, as if he knew the sadness of what he was saying. I also understood in that moment there was little he could do about it.

I went back to my hammock and couldn't get this conversation out of my head for the rest of my time in the jungle. How arrogant of me to think that I knew better, that my "environmental values" were stronger than his, that I was less "contradictory" simply because I didn't have kids to support or a sick mother to care for. Although being "poor" in the Amazon is incomparably better than being "poor" in a slum because of native peoples' ability to live off the land, their world is quickly changing. Cash is becoming a necessity, and for many native peoples, their limited means of acquiring cash present them with terrible choices.

The days of separate and distinct "indigenous" and "modern" worlds are long gone, and I began to see that any desire to keep it that way was both condescending and futile. We are all, whether we like it or not, intricately woven together, and finding ways to make our exchanges as mutually beneficial as possible seems to be the only way to approach this puzzle. The Shipibo wanted to grow and move forward as part of a globalized community. My hope was that they wouldn't have to leave their identity, their values, and the potency of their traditions behind.

It's not that I developed some righteous desire to "save" these people: if anyone was doing any saving here, they were definitely the ones saving me. But something shifted inside of me during that *dieta*. Almost three years after my first *dieta*, the plants had done a "deep clean" on me, helping to scrub out layers of fear and doubt that had accumulated on me like barnacles on the hull of a ship.

By this point I thoroughly believed in the *efficacy* of these traditions, even if I wasn't sold on any particular understanding of what "plant spirits" actually are (or aren't). I wanted to find ways to build bridges between the Amazon and the modern world and find ways to value indigenous knowledge. At that moment I didn't have any concrete ideas about how to do that beyond translating Shipibo myths, but I felt the opening of real possibility as I shed the protective shell of disillusionment that had carried me through my teenage years.

Chapter 3

Speak to the Invisible

I arrived back at Brown shortly before the fall semester of 2008 to spend some time with two of my best friends, Nat and Pat. Nat, also of Quaker descent, had spent the summer working for a clean technology investment fund in Thailand, and Pat had biked 1,500 miles across Laos, Burma, and Thailand. Every time I returned to Providence, I felt disconnected and questioned why I had come back, but sharing tales of misadventure and discovery with my friends always provided a reassuring bridge.

As we hiked through Lincoln Woods just north of the city, the conversation became very "Brown" as Nat and Pat plotted a variety of seemingly high-minded business ideas called "social enterprises" that they wanted to launch after graduation.

"So, *social enterprise,*" I asked. "Is that, like, a thing?"

"Yeah, dude," Pat said. "It's social entrepreneurship: basically, the idea that business can be used as a tool for social good by trying to find innovative methods to solve environmental or social problems in ways that nonprofits or governments suck at."

My wheels started turning.

Pat continued: "There's an economist from Bangladesh, Muhammad Yunus, who started something called Grameen Bank, which gives loans to poor people who wouldn't normally qualify. He pretty much began the whole thing. I have a book that talks about him and other social entrepreneurs I'll give you when we get back to the house."

Later that day he handed me *How to Change the World: Social Entrepreneurs and the Power of New Ideas* by David Bornstein, which tells the stories of social entrepreneurs from around the world. I started it at about 10:00 p.m. that night and finished by 5:00 the next morning, unable to put it down. After every chapter I couldn't help but reflect on the challenges I'd seen in the Amazon: the deforestation in an endless quest for hard currency, the encroachment of oil companies ever farther into the jungle, the almost impossible tightrope walked by indigenous people who wanted to preserve their traditions but also have a foot in the modern world.

Over the last few years I'd run across numerous well-intentioned nonprofits that had high hopes for saving the Amazon. Each was trying to work with local communities to protect their culture and the environment, using a variety of tactics from ecotourism, to planting some hot new commodity crop, to this nebulous concept they called "capacity building" that I could never fully wrap my head around. Unfortunately, when the tourists never showed and the global price of coffee plunged, the indigenous communities were left holding the bag.

The common denominator seemed to be that the nonprofits hadn't thought through the potential markets for the products or services they were promoting, nor had they taken a rigorous business approach to make sure that each project was actually . . . well, *sustainable* in the truest sense of the word. This social enterprise concept seemed to address some of the shortcomings of the nonprofit approach and offered me a totally new way of thinking about how you can try and make a difference.

An Energy Drink?

Brown has a "shopping period" during which you can sample classes at the start of each semester. On the first day of school I went to check out a class on social entrepreneurship that Nat had mentioned to me. My good friends Charlie Harding and Dan MacCombie were also shopping the class. When it finished, they were both heading to another business course, something called Entrepreneurship & New Ventures. It was going to be a hands-on course about building a business from the ground up. They said I should come.

My college coursework up to this point had included not a single math, science, or business class; instead, I tended to take courses like Ecopoetics, or Witchcraft in the Middle Ages—interesting, for sure, but not exactly the foundation of many thriving capitalists. I thought the social entrepreneurship class would be plenty for me, but Charlie and Dan persisted. Aden Van Noppen and Laura Thompson, two of our good friends who were also interested in international development, were also taking it, they said, and the professor was supposed to be great. I relented and decided to skip going to yoga to join them.

Danny Warshay, a successful serial entrepreneur who had cofounded and sold start-ups to companies such as Apple, was teaching the class. He told us he was going to lead the course in the style of a Harvard Business School seminar, with a focus on the practical nuts and bolts of getting a company from idea to execution. In addition to reviewing case studies in every class, the backbone for the semester would be the creation of a business plan, working in small teams to create the idea, write the plan, and then pitch it as the final.

Danny came across as such a caring, knowledgeable, and focused teacher that I forgot all my reservations about taking too many business classes and instead felt a blast of enthusiasm. The newness of the language, tone, and types of students in the class also intrigued me. I saw it as another form of cultural exploration.

Charlie, Dan, Aden, Laura, and I formed a group. We all knew each other and were friends to varying degrees. Dan and I had met the first week of freshman year (although neither one of us can remember exactly how or where, which indicates the state of mind we were probably in when we met). Charlie was a year behind us, but the three of us had all gotten close the year before in yet another quintessentially Brown class called Introduction to Contemplative Studies, in which our lab work was to meditate.

Our newly formed team came up with some really dubious business ideas over the following weeks, including an automated payment system for parking on campus, and a Fair Trade café and showroom concept. Charlie had an idea to somehow create a validation system–driver's license type thing for hitchhikers to make ridesharing easier and safer. I thought it was a terrible idea. Three months later Uber was founded with a perfect solution to essentially the same problem, just approached from the driver's side and not the traveler's side.

At the time I was trading emails with a friend in California named Jonnah. We'd hit it off after we were introduced through mutual friends over our shared interest in South America. A sweet, thoughtful, spiritually inclined guy, he had developed a passion for guayusa, the tea that I first drank in Costa Rica with Joe. Jonnah had spent time in Ecuador with an indigenous family learning more deeply about guayusa's roots. He wanted to work with that family to import and sell guayusa tea in the U.S.

I wasn't surprised by his idea. In addition to Jonnah and Joe, I had met several other people throughout my time in South America who toyed with the idea of selling guayusa in the U.S. It was an appealing concept: the tea tastes great, gives you an uncommon boost of energy, and has a deep connection to the roots of Amazonian spirituality.

The major complication was that no one had ever commercially produced guayusa. The only ways to buy guayusa at that point were from an artisans' market in Ecuador that sold piles of whole, dried leaves; from a small Ecuadorian tea company that offered a rinky-dink tea bag product; or from a few sketchy websites that sold dirty milled leaves in Ziploc bags. This meant that anyone looking to get into the far-from-burgeoning guayusa business in a serious way would have to build an entire supply chain from scratch. Not an easy task by any means, and especially hard if you were something of a hippie, as was the case of almost everyone interested in selling guayusa in the U.S. (myself included).

Given that we were having a hard time coming up with a good idea for our class, I suggested to the group that we write a business plan for Jonnah and give it to him at the end of the semester to run with. Everyone agreed.

Following Jonnah's lead, our first idea was simple: work with a few indigenous families in Ecuador who would farm the guayusa that we would then sell out of a loose-leaf tea house. Danny shook his head when we ran it by him. "Think bigger!" he ordered. Our plan, he said, sounded like a lot of work to sell a few thousand dollars' worth of tea every month. He was hyper-focused on challenging his students to craft ideas that could be scaled into large businesses.

Crammed late at night in a tiny conference room at the SciLi, one of Brown's main libraries, we brainstormed.

"Guys, what if we made a powdered guayusa product, put it in little white packets that said in big letters, 'DO NOT SNORT THIS,' and sold it on college campuses? It would crush it!" Dan joked.

"We can have different flavors, like Coco-Caine and MDMAango!" Laura said, running with it.

"THChocolate!" Charlie added, not missing a beat.

"Good morning, Mr. Venture Capitalist," Aden said, as if she was making a pitch. "Our company makes 'nasal' energy drinks inspired by hard-core drugs . . . riiiiiight."

Maybe it wasn't so far-fetched, since Four Loko, an energy drink with high amounts of caffeine, alcohol, and wormwood (the main ingredient in absinthe), was an underground success at the time—though it would soon be outlawed in several states.

"What about just making an actual energy drink?" Charlie asked.

"Sure," I laughed, thinking of aggressively in-your-face brands such as Red Bull and Monster. "That sounds like a really high-integrity social enterprise."

The rest of the group was silent, though, thinking it over. I backtracked a little. "I guess an energy drink that was actually good for you and really helps people would be something new, but isn't the idea of a healthy energy drink basically an oxymoron?"

I'd drunk a total of two Red Bulls, and both times were two of the worst nights of my life (longer stories there). As someone whose usual liquid consumption revolved around massive amounts of herbal teas such as turmeric, ginseng, hibiscus, and tulsi, consuming chemicals such as acesulfame potassium, Creatyl-L-Glutamine, and calcium disodium didn't go over too well with my body. And it certainly wasn't a product I would want to take to the market.

We did a quick Google search for "energy drinks" and one of the first images that came up was an ad that featured a zoomed-in picture of a woman's butt à la "I like big butts and I cannot lie" with a can of Monster attached to her hip, held in place by a G-string.

"Welcome to the world of energy drinks," Aden quipped.

However, a little further research revealed that we actually might be onto something: approximately $3.2 billion of energy drinks were sold in the U.S. in 2008, and the market was forecasted to grow 25 percent annually. Even better, it turned out that the other segment of the beverage industry that happened to be growing exponentially was . . . tea. Specifically, ready-to-drink teas sold in bottles and cans.

To round things out, our idea also hit the other trend sweeping the world of consumer packaged goods: we had a product with an authentic story that was organic, healthy, and made from simple and novel ingredients. As one market research report we read noted: “The major trend across all beverage categories is a new focus on the inherent goodness of a product.”

Danny’s reaction when we ran the idea by him? “That’s it!”

He was fond of citing Doug Hall, an author, entrepreneur, and consultant, who says you should identify three things when you’re thinking about starting a business: the first is the *overt benefit* your product offers; the second is that you must offer people a *real reason to believe*; the third is that there has to be a *dramatic difference* from other products on the market. If you start a business without knowing where you stand on all three of these criteria, you may succeed, but it will be much, much harder.

We’d hit all three, Danny said. We had a leaf with high amounts of caffeine that also tastes great—our *overt benefit.* The fact that the indigenous communities had used this leaf for thousands of years and that each sale of our drink would give them economic alternatives to cutting down the rainforest was *a real reason to believe.* And, finally, we would have the simplest, most natural ingredients of any energy drink on the market, which was our *dramatic difference.*

Our enthusiasm swelled as we spent more and more time on the project and many of the pieces started to fall into place. Like many of the rabbit holes I’ve launched down in my life, I can’t say my head understood what was going on, but in retrospect my heart definitely did. It took a while before I stopped to think about *why* Charlie and I started staying up most nights until 3:00 a.m. working on the business plan; *why* I stopped paying attention in my Ecopoetics class so I could finish reading about supply chain innovations at Pepsi; *why* I started drinking about a gallon of this stuff a day; *why* my ruminations and research of Amazonian plants shifted from esoteric healing plants like *ajo sacha* to things like rubber, chocolate, and soy.

I'd learned a shamanic belief that it is possible to invoke and pull different realities closer to you via techniques such as meditation and prayer. In other words, as we make our intentions explicit, we work to bring them into the world. The deeper we dove into this crazy guayusa dream, the closer I could feel its future potential.

Danny recognized our growing dedication and nudged us even further. He introduced us to Bob Burke, the former VP of sales for Stonyfield Farm yogurt, one of the first successful large-scale organic food companies. Charlie, Dan, and I drove up to Bob's home in Massachusetts to brew him some guayusa and get his take on our idea.

Bob, with his sharp, professorial manner, heard our pitch before responding. "This product is perfect for where this industry is going," he said. "Organic, sustainable, healthy products with good stories are exactly where the opportunity is. You guys could really have something here. But beverages are tough. Really, really tough."

Encouraged by his response overall—focusing more on the "really have something here" comment over the "really, really tough" part—we decided to go to the Natural Products Expo East trade show, a yearly gathering where hundreds of natural foods companies showcase their products for store buyers from across the country. The expo is not open to the public, so we posed as buyers for the Brown student café to get in. (I don't recommend subterfuge, but sometimes you have to improvise). Dan, Charlie, and I walked around gorging ourselves on samples of gluten-free cookies, almond milk, açaí juice, vegan protein powder, and these new coconut water drinks we hadn't seen before. (This was just before coconut water became "a thing.")

To our delight, we found that most of the companies brought far too much product with them for sampling and had no desire to haul it back, so we spent the last hour of the show loading Dan's car with crates of olive oil, vegan chocolate bars, organic blue corn tortilla chips, and everything in between. We did learn a handful of useful insights about key distributors and the challenges of getting new products on stores shelves, but our main takeaway was the simple pervasive positivity shared by these companies putting good, healthy products into the world.

As the end of the semester loomed, we deliriously worked on the business plan. Our final exam for Danny's course was to pitch an actual venture capitalist whom Danny invited to the class. Different VCs would come each year and Danny warned us, "Sometimes they are passive, but others can be really aggressive. Usually depends how well they slept. So be ready either way."

We stayed up nearly the whole night before the exam to hone and polish our presentation. As a result, I slept through the final exam for my social entrepreneurship class early the next morning and ended up failing the final. Ironic, I know. We walked into Danny's class as jittery as a sports team before a championship game. The venture capitalist he'd invited was from a big firm in Boston, and he sat in the front of the room in his suit and tie. It was like *Shark Tank* but without the famous rich people as judges.

Thirty seconds into the first group's presentation, the VC broke in. "What data sources did you use to confirm the size of this market?" he asked. As they stumbled to answer, he cut them off again. "I'm really just trying to assess what exactly the quantifiable market opportunity is here."

From there he interrupted about every thirty seconds with more questions. "Have you researched competitive patents for this type of product and the underlying tech?" This same degree of scrutiny and hard-core interruption also happened to the group that followed. Now our turn. We were terrified.

When thirty seconds passed and then a minute without a peep from the guy, I think we all assumed he was just gearing up for a swift, fatal punch. Finally, a minute and a half in, he spoke up.

"Excuse me," he said. Big gulps across the board from our team. "How do you all know each other?"

Of all the possible inquiries we'd prepped for, this was not on the list.

"Uh," I stammered, "We've all been friends in one way or another for quite a while . . . sir."

"Well," he said, "I can see you guys have a really special energy, a really good feeling between your team. Please continue."

"Uh, OK."

We carried on, a little bewildered, as the VC listened in silence. At the end he told us, "As you guys know, the beverage industry is really competitive. I invested in Sobe and that was a big success but a ton of work. You guys have a great idea, and I love that you're trying to help people. I wish you the best of luck."

We emerged from the classroom in a daze. We'd expected to get grilled, to be told we were fools and that our plan was laughable. Instead, the message was . . . *Go for it*? As if we actually were going to do this?

The Invisible Speaks Back

Laura had a semester left in school but already had a job lined up with Google, so she was out. Aden had recently been offered a job with Acumen Fund, a prestigious impact investing fund in New York City. Charlie and I were the ones who had latched onto the idea most, spending hours on end in my apartment brainstorming crazy business models and chugging guayusa. He was passionate about the idea but had a full year left in school and did not want to drop out. Dan and I, on the other hand, were both about to graduate in a few weeks during the mid-year graduation ceremony. Maybe, we thought, we could give it a go with Jonnah?

The decision making was complicated by the fact that Dan and I both had other desirable options. Dan had a final job interview with McKinsey the consulting firm; I had some grant opportunities to return to Peru to record, translate, and help preserve Shipibo songs. Someone might pay for me to go back and hang out with the Shipibo shamans for a year or two? I couldn't have imagined anything better.

I took to the woods that weekend and drew inward to reflect on the business concept and the bizarre idea of actually going for it. My thoughts tended toward: *You've seen the hardship in the indigenous communities. We don't live in a perfect world. While it would be amazing to go down and do your research, who is actually going to read a paper on Shipibo ethnolinguistics? What impact will it have? On the other hand, on the off chance this crackpot guayusa idea becomes something, it could make a real difference in the lives of lots of people.*

A company like the one we envisioned, I thought, could be a way to weave connections between the indigenous world and the modern world, and I liked that it would work on many levels. First and foremost, it would be a delicious product with real benefits. More deeply, I thought, over time it could be a way for Western people to learn more about indigenous traditions and for indigenous people to find a sustainable way into the world economy. If capitalism and consumerism are the languages of the modern world, I reasoned, why not find a way to address people in their native tongue?

In my grant proposals I had written about how the Shipibo use songs to transmit their ancestral knowledge of the tribe's history, mythology, and local ecology to new generations. In the same way, the Shipibo and many other indigenous tribes in the Amazonian rainforest also use plants as a foundation of their ethnic identity and teach young people about their proper identification, preparation, and use.

On the other side of the equation, I thought, much of American history and mythology is passed on to young people through brand identity—from the products people buy, the TV shows they watch, the political parties they belong to, and the sports teams they passionately support.

I was intrigued by Yogi Bhajan, who brought Kundalini yoga to the United States and began a foundation devoted to spreading its spiritual practices. In 1969 he also started Yogi Tea. It is perfectly possible to enjoy a cup of Yogi Tea without a thought to the spiritual movement behind it, and I'm sure that's what the vast majority of people do. However, those with a little more interest can find entry to a spiritual worldview via the tea, and go as deep as they wish (although there is plenty of controversy over Bhajan's integrity). I saw in our potential tea company a similar way to provide layers of access into the world of indigenous Amazonian traditions.

But as much as those heady thoughts about the possibilities for our potential company absorbed me, I was still fundamentally terrified and extremely aware of the fact that I was about the furthest thing from a businessman one could be.

Realizing I needed to shift gears from the mental knot I'd created from the intense deliberation, I reverted to the simple practice that had gotten me through many grueling experiences in the Amazon: I put my hand on my heart and reflected on everything that I was grateful for.

I felt a deep peace wash over me and was hit by a clear awareness that multiple options didn't exist: this was what we *had* to do. I remembered the feeling I'd had four months earlier at the end of my last plant *dieta* and realized this was what it had launched me toward. I felt that we were on the brink of birthing something new and positive into the world. Looking back, I honestly don't think that I would have decided to pursue the guayusa idea if I hadn't taken this time to tap into the invisible undercurrents that were less pronounced and less vocal than my fears. By letting my heart speak for me, I realized that I had no choice. Of course, my youthful ignorance must have influenced my decision making on some level too, since I had no real concept of the many, many obstacles that lay ahead in the coming years.

Dan went through his own reflective process and decided he was also in! As our graduation ceremony approached, we made plans to head to Ecuador. Now all we had to do was figure out how to get indigenous Ecuadorian farmers to grow a plant that had never been commercially produced, learn how to dry and process it, ship it to the U.S., turn it into a product, get it into stores, and compete with Coca-Cola and Red Bull . . .

Chapter 4

Finding Strength in Vulnerability

The night before we graduated from Brown in December 2008, Dan and I escaped from the frigid cold into "the Rock," the main library at Brown. With around twenty other people, we shed our clothes and ran naked through the building, handing out donuts to surprised underclassmen studying for their finals. It was part of a Brown tradition called, quite appropriately, "Naked Donuts." Since Dan and I were going to be partners in the venture—"fully exposed," if you will—there wasn't going to be much to hide in the first place.

We were vulnerable in many ways far beyond our lack of clothing. We were young, with no practical business experience and very little training, and about to head to South America to try to build a company. Naturally, we worried about failing, about letting people down, about being exposed as naïve kids with a big plan they couldn't execute.

To make it worse, three months earlier the world economy had nearly imploded in a financial crisis. The stock market was still in free fall and more than half a million jobs were being lost every month. The inauguration of Barack Obama was a month away. As we headed into graduation, we had no idea what kind of future we were stepping into or if capitalism as we knew it would survive.

During the first part of our journey, learning to transform our lack of experience and vulnerability from a liability into an asset was the key to unlocking opportunities in the uncertain world around us. Being honest about our fears and weaknesses made us available to receive the help we needed. By confidently admitting our lack of knowledge, we not only earned the trust of our partners but also inspired them to want to help us.

Originally from Chagrin Falls, Ohio, outside of Cleveland, Dan is the son of two psychologists and the stepson, grandson, and nephew to four social workers. His tendencies toward self-reflection and personal growth were deeply ingrained. Dan sadly lost his mother at the age of eleven and spent much of his childhood adventuring in the woods around his house, seeking connection and solace in the natural world. He went on to raise brook trout and maintain a maple sugar bush while in high school.

A lifelong fascination with the ocean and an early love of snorkeling led Dan to major in marine biology at Brown. He also spent time working in the state legislature to reform access to medical services and led writing workshops in Rhode Island prisons. During a semester off, he visited South America, where he hiked the Andes, went scuba diving in the Galápagos Islands, and worked with an indigenous chocolate cooperative in the Ecuadorian Amazon.

Dan loved to recite a quote often attributed to John Muir, "When one tugs at a single thing in nature, he finds it attached to the rest of the world." Dan's passion for social justice and environmental conservation inspired him to think constantly about the basic role that people have in taking care of the world around them.

As they arrived in Rhode Island for the graduation ceremony, my parents—despite my mom's love of travel and my dad's entrepreneurial streak—were not exactly convinced that moving to South America to start an Amazonian tea company was the wisest move.

After the ceremony, as we stood eating appetizers under oil paintings of former Brown presidents and benefactors in Salomon Hall, my entrepreneurship professor, Danny Warshay, came up to meet my parents. My dad pulled him to the side and asked, "Are you really sure this is a good idea?"

"They're good kids, and the idea is certainly a good one," Danny said. "And, really, they have nothing to lose, even if this fails—which, of course, odds are that it will."

I'm not sure that was what my dad wanted to hear.

Our original plan was also shifting. Our relationship with Jonnah had deteriorated as we became excited about jumping into the business with him. Jonnah wanted to do something more artisanal and small-scale, whereas we were thinking bigger.

Eventually we decided to go our separate ways and wished each other well. Dan and I made sure to send him all our business plan materials, projections, and associated research to make good on our original commitment. It was not only the right thing to do, but we figured that the existence of two guayusa companies instead of one could potentially help more indigenous people benefit from growing guayusa and build a bigger market in the U.S. at the same time. In the end, though, he never took any further steps.

Meet the Shiguangos

A few days after Christmas, I was on a plane to Ecuador for the very first time. (Even though I'd spent extensive time in Peru and Brazil, I had never made it this far north on the continent.) As I rode in a taxi from the airport, I got my first look at Quito, Ecuador's capital, located at 9,300 feet, a low-rise sprawl of nearly two million people spread across a valley surrounded by the jutting peaks of several Andean volcanoes.

I met up with Dan, Charlie, and Laura at a hostel in the old, colonial-era part of Quito. Although Laura had another semester before heading to work for Google, and Charlie had a year left in school, they'd decided to come down during winter break to help us get started.

The hostel was not the ideal place for people looking to start an ambitious business. It was four stories, with a bar on the top floor full of backpackers on the "Gringo Trail": a mix of students taking semesters off from college, Europeans and Australians enjoying long holidays, and assorted spiritual seekers. We slept in a room crowded with four bunk beds. Romance and partying were clearly the priorities for our fellow guests.

We'd arrived in Ecuador with a decidedly short list of contacts and leads: exactly two. The first had come through the Myspace site (yes, Myspace) that Jonnah had set up. A month before graduation, we received a very excited one-paragraph email from a man in Ecuador named Ricardo Shiguango, who wrote that his community had dreamed of sharing guayusa with the world and would like to work with us.

We'd learned that Ricardo was Kichwa, part of the largest indigenous group in Latin America. There are some ten million Quechua in Argentina, Bolivia, Chile, Colombia, Peru, and also Ecuador, where the preferred spelling and pronunciation is "Kichwa" (pronounced "Keech-wa").

The most typical image someone might have of the Quechua is probably an indigenous person in Peru or Bolivia dressed in colorful clothes and holding a llama by the reins, but the group is far more diverse. Once many ethnicities, they were all colonized and strategically assimilated by the Incas beginning in the 1400s, and all now speak the Incan language—known as Runashimi, Quechua, or Kichwa (sometimes spelled Quichua).

Even in Ecuador there are several discrete Kichwa subgroups, with the main dividing line lying between the Kichwa who live in the Andes region and those in the Amazon. In Ecuador, the Kichwa make up about 2.5 million of the country's 16 million people. Most of those are Andean Kichwa. Ricardo Shiguango was Amazonian Kichwa, a subgroup with a population of sixty thousand people, making them a distinct minority even within their broader indigenous group.

We met Ricardo a few days after we arrived in Quito, at an Internet café on the second floor of a downtown building. We sat around a table with coffees as motorbikes buzzed by on the street below and young men wearing headphones played first-person shooter video games on the café's computers. Pop music blared from speakers mounted on the wall. Charlie and I, much to Dan and Laura's chagrin, happened to have a rich appreciation for Ke$ha's masterpieces, so we felt right at home.

Ricardo was short, in his late thirties, and obviously very happy to meet a few Americans interested in selling guayusa. He wore khaki pants and a button-down shirt that we could tell, from his lack of comfort in them, weren't his preferred way to dress. The meeting had the same awkward feeling as online dating.

Over time, we learned that Ricardo and his brother Alejandro had long been hustling to make some opportunities for themselves. Some years before, they had hooked up with a group of Americans that tried to develop ecotourism in their village, an effort that in the end failed to bear fruit. However, it was clear even from a few minutes of conversation that Ricardo was truly passionate about guayusa.

After chatting for around thirty minutes, he said, "Come out to my community and meet my parents. We'll drink guayusa!"

Ignoring what would surely have been our own parents' advice to avoid wandering off into the jungle with strangers we'd met on the Internet, we agreed. Our friend Nat was fond of the saying "The universe provides," and that seemed to be exactly what was happening. Also, we had nothing else going on.

The next day we all got on a bus and headed out of Quito, and I got the first of what would become a familiar experience: the television at the front playing kung fu and action movies (Jean-Claude Van Damme and Jerry Bruckheimer are both national treasures) and the lurching to and fro as the driver aggressively tailgated, slammed the gas and the brakes (sometimes at once), and pulled out to pass on blind corners.

Ecuador is about the same size as the state of New Mexico, but it includes four separate geographic zones—the Galápagos Islands, which sit 600 miles off the shoreline; the Pacific coast at the Western edge; the Andes, which run up the center of the country; and the Amazon rainforest in the east.

Leaving Quito by road is always spectacular. The city is ringed by volcanoes, and the landscape on the outskirts is barren, dusty, and dry. The road then quickly plunges, and during about four hours of switchbacks, you drop from 9,300 feet to 1,500 feet. Suddenly you are in the lush green surroundings of the Upper Amazon. The air thickens and sticks in your lungs, and the heat and humidity coat your skin. It's as if it were fifty miles from Denver to the Everglades.

Ricardo lived in the Pastaza Province, southeast of Quito. It took us a couple hours to reach Puyo, a pop-up, grungy industrial town of thirty thousand. From there we caught a local bus, which jostled over a dirt road flanked by jungle, until we reached Pindo, Ricardo's village, which consisted of several huts and a big dirt field. There were about twenty-five people living in the village, and most wandered between houses in such a way that it was hard to tell who owned what or whose kids were whose.

Ricardo introduced us to his father, Gustavo, the family patriarch. Around seventy, short and wiry, with a mischievous air, he made it clear he was in charge. He greeted us very formally, which is a common trait among Kichwa elders. His preferred method of address, for example, was always *Estimado* (which translates to "Dear" or "Esteemed") and then your name. It was hard for him to remember Western names, however, so as long as we stayed with him, he had a habit of saying "*Estimado . . . eh . . . este, este . . .*" and then waiting for someone to cue him to the name of the person he was addressing.

He welcomed us warmly. "I've had visions of people from the north who come to bring guayusa to the world," he said.

We took this as a good sign.

Later that afternoon Ricardo's older brother, Alejandro, showed up. Unlike Ricardo, who always exhibited some social anxiety, Alejandro was gregarious and charismatic, and wore a long ponytail that reached halfway down his back. Alejandro was a natural storyteller, one of the best I've ever come across. For example, he soon told us a story about the origin of the moon. He said a woman named Iluku was secretly impregnated by her brother. The two tried to escape their village together, but he rose up to the sky while she remained on earth. She transformed into a potoo bird and longingly sang "*Ilukuuu*" (which is the potoo bird's call) to her lost lover in the night sky. Alejandro jumped, crouched, pranced, glowered, and even squatted to imitate the bird while he told the story, which made it quite irresistible. He quickly nudged Ricardo to the side in capturing our time and attention.

The Shiguango family set us up in one of the huts they'd built for the failed ecotourism venture and began to teach us about their village. It was a typical Amazonian Kichwa community in that the people living there were still struggling to find their place in the modern economy: they were trying to keep their traditions but also had to make a living. They farmed crops such as corn, worked as migrant laborers, and chopped and sold wood.

Shortly after we dropped our backpacks, they ushered us

to visit their *chakra*, bustling with verdant guayusa trees. The *chakras* are "forest gardens"; they'd be called "permaculture" or "agroforestry" in American terminology. Typically, they include dozens of plants all growing haphazardly together in what might appear to be just any chunk of rainforest. But the *chakra* contains an intentional mix of everything people need: staples such as yucca, plantains, bananas, beans, and peanuts; medicinal plants such as *churiyuyu* (used to heal cuts), *shia* (an anesthetic), and *bagarimandi* (a plant they say helps men to attract females); and trees such as red cedar, balsa, and pilche, whose fruit is a gourd.

You could think of the *chakra* as a sort of strategically managed swatch of rainforest, where the Kichwa machete down any species they don't want and create space for the useful ones to grow at their leisure. It is a totally sustainable system of agriculture that requires no fertilizers or pesticides, where water filtration, soil enrichment, pest control, and wildlife habitat protection are all taken care of by nature itself.

When we arrived in Pindo, a few guayusa trees were actually flowering with beautiful purple petals. Gustavo said this was a very rare occurrence and told us it was a favorable sign for our business prospects. Having now seen thousands and thousands of guayusa trees, I've only seen them flower one other time since then.

To harvest guayusa, they plucked off the roughly six-by-two-inch leaves, stacked about twenty of them together, folded the resulting leaf packet in half, and pierced it through the middle onto a thin vine. By adding more and more leaf packets, they created a bright wreath of guayusa, which they hung on a post near the fire.

Each morning, leaf packets were ripped off as needed to add to the guayusa pot. On harvest days the tea was very fresh and tasted lighter, more vegetal. As time passed and the leaves dried over the fire, it became dark and smoky.

Sleeping in to rest after a long trip and jet lag wasn't even close to being a possibility: at 3:00 a.m. Gustavo barged into our hut and boldly proclaimed "Guayusa!"

After stumbling down to the main hut, we encountered Gustavo, Ricardo, Alejandro, their wives, kids, as well as aunts, uncles, and various cousins, wide-awake, chatting, laughing, nursing, and weaving *shigras* (traditional palm fiber bags).

There was a defined etiquette to the ceremony. The women were the only ones who could make the tea, boiling leaves over a fire in a ceremonial pot made of red river clay. When it was ready, they scooped it up with special gourds and poured it back and forth from gourd to gourd, cooling and aerating it, sometimes while doing a little dance.

We packed onto wooden benches that were arranged around the fire. I quickly saw the practical role guayusa plays in the ritual. I dealt with the discomfort and the lack of sleep by chugging as much tea as I needed to jolt myself into consciousness, feeling pleasantly alert and energized when it began to kick in.

When we were all arranged and had gourds in hand, we began to share our dreams, which Gustavo and Alejandro interpreted.

The guayusa ceremony is an ancient tradition, possibly thousands of years old, and the dream interpretation is not like Freudian analysis. Whereas Freud believed that dreams presented clues into the individual unconscious, the Kichwa see dreams as insight into both the collective unconscious and the spirit world, offering practical guidance from realms beyond our own.

It's hard as a Westerner to fully wrap one's head around Kichwa ideas about dreams. A core belief is that individual dreams can be part of a bigger whole, so that they are often interwoven into a greater story. If Maria dreamt of thunder and Ricardo dreamt of a turtle coming out of a river, the combination of the two dreams could mean that the *watusa* (the agouti, the large jungle rodent they hunt) would be on top of the hills at sunset that day.

I could never figure out an associative logic behind the interpretations, but the family members always seemed perfectly convinced of the intended meaning, as if reading definitions from a dictionary. If someone saw the headwaters of a river rising in a dream, it could mean a visitor was coming, but it could also mean someone was going to get sick. A dream of a particular "Spirit Owner of the Lightning" meant that it was going to be a good season for a certain type of ant they liked to eat, beginning the day after tomorrow. Other dreams contained guidance about where to hunt for certain animals, or warnings that someone was in danger.

Beyond the dream interpretation, the guayusa ceremony was a way for everyone to connect at the start of the day. Alejandro recounted tales about the history and mythology of the Kichwa, we sang songs, and often just shared stories about whatever was on our minds. Although getting up at three in the morning was never fun to start the day, we began to see the guayusa ceremony as something that contributed, on the most fundamental level, to the psychological health of the community, giving people a space to bond with others. Taking part in the ceremony made everyone feel they had a role in the well-being of the group.

This is not to say that everything was perfect or that people had no problems, but there was a genuine and unmistakable feeling of warmth and openness. Given our typical American upbringings, in which some level of depression and anxiety are really the norm, this was both refreshing and eye-opening.

It amazed me to hear Alejandro, with his captivating imitations of plant and animal spirits—full of onomatopoeic *zing!*- and *oooof!*- and *ka-TING!*–type sounds—tell stories about his family and their relation to the land that went back hundreds of years. I was hardly aware of my history beyond my grandparents, and certainly had never heard stories passed down over ten or more generations. And I did not see the plants growing outside my childhood home as living entities with their own stories to tell.

"Guayusa Is Our Blood"

After a few days Ricardo, Alejandro, and Gustavo took Dan, Charlie, Laura, and me deep into the jungle, which was humid and staggeringly hot. Alejandro cleared the trail with his machete. Both of the brothers carried rifles, although we never figured out if it was to protect us from other humans or for hunting. We preferred not to think about it.

This part of the Amazon is a particularly special zone where the jungle meets the foothills of the Andes. Known as the Pestaña de la Selva, or "Eyelash of the Jungle," it is one of the most biodiverse regions in the world. Scientists have documented 150 different types of amphibians in the area, 600 bird species, and 1,100 types of trees (compared to 655 types of trees in all of North America).

As we walked, we saw trails of leaf-cutting ants, termite mounts, toucans perched in trees, and hawks soaring above. Alejandro and Ricardo often stopped and pulled leaves off plants, telling us to chew this or rub that on our skin: one was good for stomachaches, another for fevers.

This location, where the jungle meets the mountains—a liminal, in-between sort of a world—has shaped the Amazonian Kichwa's identity and culture. It has made them very intercultural, as historically they have traded between the indigenous groups who live deeper in the Amazon, those up in the Andes, and, more recently, Europeans. It's placed them at the center of fights over deforestation, usurpation of land for settlers, and the expansion of oil companies. Guayusa is also endemic to this area: the "Eyelash of the Jungle" is the only place in the world where it is found.

After several hours, we reached a little shack with bamboo walls and a plastic tarp for a roof. In the distance, the seventeen-thousand-foot snowcapped peak of the Sangay volcano rose from the Andes.

We camped for three nights, spending the days hiking, swimming, and talking. Alejandro entertained us with Kichwa legends, his ponytail swinging behind him as he jumped and gesticulated. One night we stayed up late telling stories and discussing visions for how guayusa could reach the world. Then late turned into early, and—rather than entertaining the idea of sleep (even though we were dozing off between tales)—the guayusa pot went on the fire and the day started.

One story Alejandro told was of the origin of guayusa.

In the old times, he said, humans didn't know how to dream, which left them isolated in the physical world, without access to other realms. One day a hunter was out in the jungle when it started to rain. He took cover in the expansive, ten-foot-tall roots of an enormous copal tree and dozed off. A mushroom spirit appeared to him and said, "Someone from the village needs to take a long trip downriver, and you will learn how to dream."

Back in the village, the elders chose two smart and rambunctious fourteen-year-old twins to make the trip, sending them off in a canoe. After a week of travel, they pulled over to sleep on a beach. At dusk they saw a gleaming white city of temples on the other side.

When they crossed the river, the mushroom spirit appeared and escorted them up a spiral staircase into the realm of the heavenly sky people, where they saw the village ancestors lined up along with plant spirits, jaguars, and anacondas. The mushroom spirit handed them a wreath of guayusa and said, "Take this back to your people, and it will teach you how to dream."

They paddled back, and the villagers drank the tea and started to dream. Their hunting and fishing improved because they were more connected to the jungle, more awake, alert, and protected. Their intuition sharpened and they could see where game would be, and started to understand how other plants could be used as medicine. Unfortunately, they quickly used up the whole supply and had to send the twins back downriver to get more.

This time, when they got back to the place where there had been the city of light, they instead found a grove of ancient trees arranged in a tight circle. In the middle they discovered a guayusa plant. They cut off a few branches, which they brought back to the village and planted, bringing guayusa to humans once and for all. (Guayusa remains infertile on its own and must be planted by humans to propagate.)

Since then, Alejandro told us, guayusa has been the anchor plant of the Kichwa people. Its influence went far beyond delivering a jolt of caffeine that helped them stay awake during long hunts. In fact, it became the Amazonian Kichwa's primary plant ally. It has opened them up to a deeper connection with their ancestors and the world of the spirits, which in turn has facilitated personal "introductions," if you will, to other medicine plants.

It is, Alejandro said, echoing a sentiment I've heard from other Amazonian Kichwa many times since, the animating force, the foundation, of their culture: "Guayusa is our blood."

We wondered if the Kichwa would object to their most sacred plant being commercialized and introduced to the outside world, but Alejandro and Ricardo were the first to insist that wasn't the case. Before our hike back to Pindo, Ricardo decided he needed to do something to "seal" the great experience we'd had in the jungle, since our minds and spirits had become very open, he said. It was ten in the morning and already blazing hot under the tarp, especially since we'd had a fire going for several hours. The persistent multitude of insects that buzzed around and landed on us made things even more uncomfortable.

Ricardo took some coals out of the fire with his bare hands and had Dan kneel down in front of him. He then blew smoke all around Dan's face and vigorously slapped the top of his head with both hands. This went on quite a while before he moved on to Laura and me. Charlie was the last to go. He had a buzz cut and had developed an intense sunburn on his scalp when we were at the river the day before, so Ricardo's hot slapping was far from welcome.

Alejandro had been out wandering around when Ricardo started the ritual. He returned during Charlie's turn, observed for a moment, and then announced that Ricardo was doing it wrong. He elbowed his brother to the side and proceeded to give Charlie the same treatment for another ten minutes.

From what we could tell, Alejandro did not do it any differently from Ricardo. From Charlie's expression, it was obvious that he, a generally stoic New Englander, had had enough. In the photo we took, however, he looks very serene and mystical—the gringo visitor receiving a traditional blessing from his indigenous hosts.

The danger would be a tendency to fall into one-way exchanges where either the Americans were seen as having all the answers or the "unspoiled" indigenous people were viewed as having some kind of mystical solution. What we would have to step into was a constant cultural give-and-take, in the same way the Amazonian Kichwa people have swayed and twirled with outsiders for centuries as a basic means of survival.

A Liberal Arts Approach to Business

We left Pindo very excited, feeling that the Shiguango brothers were potential business partners and that our prospects were looking up.

Charlie and Laura departed, leaving Dan and me to turn

to our only other contact in Ecuador, Yolanda Kakabadse, a former minister of the environment who would soon become president of the World Wildlife Fund. We connected with her through the mother of a teaching assistant in one of Dan's classes at Brown who had served with her on the board of the Ford Foundation, proving it is definitely worth mining every potential connection you have.

We met Yolanda at her apartment in one of Quito's nicest neighborhoods, riding the elevator up to her spacious, light-filled apartment, where we took in the view of the city's sprawl. Yolanda immediately put us at ease: she was intellectual, worldly, and charismatic, but also radiant and kind. In one of the first of many strange coincidences since we committed to bringing guayusa to the world market, Yolanda turned out to be a huge fan of the plant already.

This was totally unexpected: guayusa is not a common drink among Ecuadorians besides the Amazonian Kichwa. Yolanda, who had long worked on environmental issues, told us that she discovered it when meeting with Kichwa communities thirty years earlier and had drunk it every day since. A woman in a local indigenous market would hook her up with leaves, and she always carried a thermos of guayusa. She credited it with helping her through menopause and boosting her immune system. She nicknamed Dan and me "*mis guayusas*" ("my guayusas").

Despite the good vibes, Yolanda's tone changed after we'd spoken awhile, becoming more somber. The message was clear: she was willing to put some of her goodwill on the line to help us, but we had better not let her down. There was little Dan and I could do but assure her of our resolve.

Yolanda set us up with a list of contacts in the Ecuadorian

government and large nonprofits. We promised we would get in touch with all her contacts within a few weeks. Rather than slapping our heads with coals before we left, she gave us sweet kisses on the sides of our cheeks, and said, "If you're actually going to do this, do it." Then she added half jokingly, "If you move back to the U.S. in three months, I'll personally come track you down."

Dan and I left Yolanda's apartment excited but overwhelmed. Neither of us had any practical business preparation besides Danny Warshay's class. Dan's thesis had been on marsh crab habitats in New England. Mine had been a magical realist novel.

Since the only thing we had known up to that point in our lives was applying ourselves in school, we decided that, rather than trying to pass ourselves off as business experts, we would stick to our strengths and approach our work exactly like what we were: liberal arts students. We knew how to research, ask questions, and process information from sometimes contradictory sources, and figured that this spirit of learning could get us at least a few miles down the road.

In the months following the meeting with Yolanda, we threw ourselves into learning everything we could, both meeting with people in person and maniacally reading about Ecuador, the history of indigenous federations there, agroforestry, Fair Trade, and everything in between. Over time, this approach helped us develop the framework for how we eventually built Runa.

We learned, among other things, the history of the indigenous people in Ecuador and their complicated place in its politics. In the 1460s the Incans colonized a large swath of the country, only to be overrun in 1534 by the Spanish, who were helped by some local indigenous tribes rebelling against Inca rule. The Spanish began the social hierarchy that still predominates in the country today—the small percentage descended from the Spanish make up the upper class, below which lies mixed-race *mestizos*, and then the indigenous people. Exact numbers are impossible to come by, but it's thought around 10 to 20 percent of Ecuadorians are "white," 40 to 55 percent are *mestizos*, and 25 to 40 percent are indigenous.

The indigenous people along the coast and in the Andean region have traditionally been at the economic bottom, first as indentured labor on farms owned by the Spanish upper classes, and later in similar positions on cacao and banana plantations. Those in the Amazon have remained largely untouched until relatively recently.

The rubber boom of the early 1900s brought fortune hunters, missionaries, and development into the jungle. Modern demands for timber, arable land, and most of all oil have transformed the Amazon. The discovery of oil in the Ecuadorian Amazon in the 1960s has led to exploration and production deeper and deeper into the jungle, with the indigenous groups either getting pushed off their lands or being poisoned by pollution. At this point about *half* of Ecuador's total GNP comes from oil, giving foreign petroleum companies massive leverage to get what they want from the government; a collapse in oil revenues poses a constant threat to civil stability.

The indigenous communities have not passively accepted the situation. In the 1980s they began to organize into federations to fight for their political interests, becoming the first registered indigenous federations in the world. These groups have been active, staging several uprisings in the 1990s that blocked all roads into Quito to demand political reforms. In January

2000, twenty thousand indigenous people marched to Quito. In concert with sympathetic military officers, the indigenous leadership overthrew the national government and deposed the president. For a period of less than a day, a three-person junta, including Antonio Vargas, an Amazonian Kichwa leader, ruled Ecuador.

This wasn't just academic background for us. The Shiguangos had been very active in trying to push back against oil company encroachment on Kichwa land. They were also friends with Antonio Vargas, and we ate lunch with him on occasion. This was still a relatively militant community, and in starting our company we had to be aware of this history of exploitation and be mindful of our Kichwa partners' natural suspicions about our motives.

Working to gain a deeper understanding of this backdrop, we tried to meet with everyone we could, sending up to eighty introductory emails a day to government officials, academics, business people, indigenous leaders, nonprofit directors, botanists, and forestry experts.

One of the core lessons I learned from the Shipibo was that invoking things can be easy, but tolerating the consequences can often be brutal. Pouring a few ounces of a plant brew down your throat is simple, but swimming in Pandora's box for the next five to twenty-five hours is a different story. In the same way, anyone can say they are going to start a business, but actually doing it means you have to be willing to trudge aimlessly through the mud.

This attitude was essential, because our early welcome from the Shiguango family in Pindo gave us a false sense of how we were going to be greeted. As we got to know the country, we visited around twenty other Kichwa communities. These were villages much like Pindo, typically home to anywhere from 25 to 150 people.

When we told them we wanted to buy guayusa for cash and sell it in the U.S., the reaction was often quite harsh. Imagine a dozen or so people sitting, listening acutely, pausing for a minute with blank faces, and then bursting into hysterical laughter. This wasn't normal chuckling, either, but more like cackling: the Kichwa can laugh in a way that is pure unrestrained mirth, with the women almost shrieking. When they calmed down, they would talk among themselves in Kichwa. One might ask in Spanish: "You give us actual money just for guayusa leaves? And sell it where? *In the United States of America?*" Then the merriment would start again.

After the laughter subsided and we explained that, no, this wasn't a joke, the conversations became serious. We received one consistent message: *Don't fuck with us.*

We heard about the many failed development projects that had been foisted on the Kichwa and were shown plots of land where abandoned coffee trees, planted at the encouragement of foreigners, were being overtaken by the jungle, since many families gave up coffee production when prices tanked. In one form or another, we heard: *We don't want false promises and expectations, and we don't know if we trust you guys. We don't need any more NGOs coming here to lecture us or to teach us nebulous skills we're not actually going to use.*

The local leaders were very clear. *What we need is for people to buy our stuff,* they said. *We need money for all the things we can't grow. We think what you are doing is kind of crazy, but if you can do that, and generate income for our people, we'll be happy to work with you.*

By admitting that we didn't have a clear vision for how to effectively partner with these communities and just listening to their ideas and feedback, we confidently invoked our vulnerability. We clearly stated that we weren't there to "help" but that our simple hope was to partner in building a business that could grow and profit all of us. Thankfully, they responded with equal transparency and respect, defining for us what a successful partnership would look like.

Three-Month Goals

After several months of running around, most often separately to maximize the amount of ground we could cover, Dan and I needed a break.

Baños de Agua Santa, a tourist town in the jungle at the base of the Andes, seemed perfect. In addition to the thermal baths that give the town its name, you can also go rafting, bungee jump, and hike to waterfalls.

Despite the "Shit, we're in this together"–type support we offered each other, things weren't always peachy and it was important that Dan and I have some downtime together. We are both very different personalities, and in our work we tended to go in the direction of our interests. He was an excellent photographer, and if we went hiking, he loved to snap pictures, look around, stare at spiders, and take some time to enjoy and absorb.

I always wanted to get somewhere—my longstanding competitive streak still alive and well—and I'd often prefer to go for a long run up through the woods to tire myself out, covering as much ground as I could.

In business, this created a useful dynamic. If my tendency was to push things a little too fast, Dan's was to be more deliberate and analyze them. Between the two of us, we usually came to a suitable meeting point in the middle.

In Baños, we tried to relax in thermal swimming pools crowded with Ecuadorian families on vacation, sliding in among the grandmas and the toddlers. At night we hit the bars, drinking bottles of Pilsener, Ecuador's very watery national beer.

The task ahead was suddenly getting very real. I had just learned that I'd been approved for a Fulbright scholarship to study Shipibo songs and language. Turning it down made me realize that even with all the doors that were opening for us, some were also closing. My vision of becoming an academic who studied and wrote about Amazonian culture was potentially slipping away.

The tone of the conversations between Dan and me was also transitioning from academic inquiry to business logistics. We were grappling with the immensity of what lay ahead: We had to organize farmers to start producing guayusa for commercial use; we had to design and build a factory; we had to export guayusa to the United States; we had to develop a brand and packaging; we had to get it into stores; and before we could do any of it, we had to raise the capital to fund it all.

Beyond that, I had just read the World Bank's *Doing Business* report that assesses the ease of conducting business in foreign countries and ranks countries from most to least favorable. Ecuador was near the bottom of the list, number 136 out of 180, with Syria occupying number 137 and Uzbekistan at number 138.

The only way we were going to be able to handle the pressure, we realized, was to focus on the immediate weeks ahead and ask one question: What do we have to do in these next three months to avoid calling our parents and asking them to buy us plane tickets home?

Whatever big challenge you might face, I can't recommend this approach enough. It allowed us to forget the overwhelming challenge ahead and focus on smaller, achievable tasks. For example, in three months we could make connections with the national indigenous federation, figure out what we needed to do to get an export license, and hire a local team member. Three months later we would set another short list of goals for the following ninety days.

In the end, it helped grow the business in ways we hadn't anticipated. Often, in the early days, people we spoke with assumed we were nice college kids having an adventure before running back to the U.S.

When we got that reception, we simply shared the goals we had set for the coming months. When we met our targets, we got back in touch with those people, let them know about our progress, and told them our goals for the next three months. After a while they couldn't help but admit that these kids were actually getting things done. This persistence and proven focus helped us land some of our earliest outside investors as well.

What's in a Name?

After several months in Ecuador, we were introduced to an Amazonian Kichwa man named Virgilio. We were told he had worked for several NGOs and was very committed to conservation, sustainability, and the preservation of Kichwa traditions. He lived a few hours from Quito, in Napo Province, just north of Pastaza, where we had stayed with the Shiguangos.

Virgilio's family lived in a small village outside the town of Archidona. It had a totally different feel from Pastaza, which had been exploited more profoundly in the preceding decades by outsiders for oil and timber. Archidona, a colonial town founded by the Spanish in 1560, never had a big boom: it was still a sleepy jungle hideaway.

We felt an instant connection with Virgilio. In his thirties, he was positive, fun, and thoughtful. His dad, Don Ernesto, was in his nineties and a revered shaman and healer. As a kid, Virgilio had done very well in school but had also been something of a rebel. He had taken up boxing and become very good, in part because his dad supplied him with performance-enhancing shamanic plants, such as *yacu yutzu* bark, that gave him energy.

Virgilio won Ecuador's youth boxing title and was set to go to the South American championship when he learned it was scheduled for the same weekend as his high school graduation test that would determine where he would go to college. There was no makeup for the test. Virgilio knew education was his chance to do something for his people, so he skipped the boxing championship.

Although his dad was a shaman, Virgilio, like many indigenous youths in Ecuador, did not fully sign on to the traditional belief systems. After college, when he started working on conservation issues, Virgilio began to have recurring dreams in which he was bitten by a snake. His dad had the same dreams and warned Virgilio, but Virgilio was convinced the premonition meant nothing and ignored it.

One day, deep in the Yasuní National Park and Biosphere Reserve, where he was doing tree measurements for a conservation group, a highly venomous viper bit Virgilio on the shoulder. He had to be airlifted to Quito and barely survived. From that point he accepted that it could be possible to get guidance from dreams and started to use them as tools.

Virgilio also introduced us to his friend Oscar, a local forestry engineer, and we clicked immediately. Given their combined experience with organic cacao and coffee projects, we decided they were the perfect guys to start up our operation in Napo, organize farmers, and begin propagating more guayusa trees.

At the same time, we began working more seriously in Pastaza. Alejandro had introduced us to Luis Yumbo, who had run one of the largest indigenous federations in the Amazon. In his fifties, he was very connected. We really wanted his experience and network, so we hired him to be our regional manager. The fact that he was very smooth in the style of a politician, had no business or forestry experience, and didn't have his own email address probably should have given us pause.

Alejandro stayed in constant contact. His preferred method was to call me at three or four in the morning when we were in Quito (sleeping, of course), excited to tell me some news or idea that had just occurred to him.

One morning I picked up to hear his usual greeting, "*¡Hola, Thai-lor! ¿Cómo estás, mi estimado hermano?*" ("Hi, Tyler! [They never could get a handle on my name. It was either Thai-lor or Tee-lair.] How are you my dear brother?")

"I'm fine, Alejandro," I mumbled. "What's up?"

"I've had a vision for the name of the company!"

Of course, he wouldn't tell me what it was: the only appropriate way to reveal his vision, he said, would be during a guayusa ceremony. Classic Alejandro.

Up to this point the name had stumped us. We'd tossed around some pretty terrible ideas, such as Blue Jaguar, which could either be Ron Burgundy's cologne in *Anchorman* or the blatant attempt to copy Red Bull that it was. We had also entertained a variety of Kichwa words we'd learned but didn't know enough about them, nor did we feel comfortable being the ones to place a Kichwa name on the business.

We'd already planned to go back to Pindo in a couple days. Our first morning there, Alejandro filled us in. "A woman came to me in a dream and said four words," he told us. "*Sinchi Sacha Warmi Runa!*"

"Um, *Sinchi Sacha Warmi Runa*?" we asked.

"Yes," Alejandro said, "that's the name of the company!"

"Um, OK. Uh, what's it mean?" I asked.

Alejandro translated: "*Sinchi* is 'strong.' *Sacha* means 'wild forest.' *Warmi* is 'female energy.' *Runa* means a 'fully alive person.' "

He put it together: "Strong Forest Women Fully Alive People Energy."

Dan and I hesitated. "Yeah, um, Alejandro you know that some Americans have kind of short attention spans, so four words might be just a tad too much," I said. But "Runa" was actually a word on our short list of potential names, which we thought simply meant "person," so I asked him to tell us more about its meaning.

"Runa," Alejandro said, "is the spirit and essence of our identity. It means to be aware and awake, to be alive in the present and to respect our ancestors, to live in harmony with the rainforest, to be a piece of creation with agency and creativity.

A person, an animal, or plant, they can all be Runa. There are jaguar Runa and tree Runa, too. If you are Runa it means you are fully creating with life, knowing your role in this world and in the world of dreams."

For the Kichwa, Alejandro explained, guayusa was integral to reaching this state. "We drink guayusa to become Runa," he said.

Dan and I looked at each other and just knew that was it. It offered a richness of spirit and a connection to life, central to what we aimed to achieve with our business. We also knew that Runa was meant to be about people: improving livelihoods for farmers and providing a healthy product to consumers.

We also learned to appreciate the name on a deeper level as time went on. We found that Ecuadorians who were not Kichwa laughed when we told them we were calling our company "Runa." The word, we learned, was slang for "mutt dog" or "something that has no value, something worthless." The Spanish had used "Runa" as a slur to describe the Kichwa, seeing them as "mutts"—not of "purebred" Spanish descent.

This racist, discriminatory adoption of the word had become so embedded in the culture that, sadly, most Ecuadorians had no idea of the original meaning. We felt that, by taking "Runa" as our name, it was a small step toward helping to reclaim that heritage as something valuable, something worthwhile. Also, two gringo kids educating *quiteño* cabdrivers about what the word "Runa" actually means was always hilarious.

Invigorated by our newly discovered identity, we began to pick up speed in the coming months. We received great news from Charlie in the U.S.: we'd won two separate business plan competitions, one sponsored by Brown University, the other by the state of Rhode Island. The combined prizes came out to $70,000 in seed money. With this cash in hand we could now get to work for real.

When we got to Ecuador, we clearly had no idea what was going to happen. By being willing to embrace our vulnerability and act like students instead of business experts, we opened ourselves up to conversations in which we were met with respect and excitement. We learned that it's hard for anyone to criticize you for being uninformed or inexperienced if you're the first one to say you don't know anything! Especially in the world of business, vulnerability is usually considered a curse, but this misperception can be quite disempowering. Vulnerability is not about being weak; it's about having courage to be honest with yourself. Finding strength in vulnerability is about using that honesty and humility to ask for and get help where you need it. We often tend to hide or deny our weaknesses and vulnerabilities, thereby creating a blind spot that actually makes you weak. Instead of avoiding and pretending like we don't have weaknesses or we don't lack information, we can proactively admit our limitations, learn what we don't know, and invite support, which we always need in one way or another.

Additionally, this attitude helped us build relationships. From an indigenous point of view, "knowledge" isn't particularly valuable when it's just an isolated set of facts. The act of sharing and receiving information is what breathes power into it. With our earnest curiosity and willingness to be transformed and directed by who and what we encountered, it seemed that people became even more willing to share with us.

There was more power in these exchanges than any of us could have harnessed as individuals. Just as the Kichwa people understand that it can take multiple people's dreams to tell one cohesive story, so too did we learn that a resilient business model is one that weaves together many different ideas offered by a diversity of stakeholders. Drinking from the same pots of guayusa, walking the same trails, and hearing each other's stories somehow seemed to clear the path for the intangible "dream" of Runa to begin to coalesce into reality.

Chapter 5

Business as Ceremony

The unexpected infusion of cash meant we could actually start developing guayusa production for real. As much as we loved learning and immersing ourselves in the heritage of guayusa, we were now facing the challenges of putting our ideas into practice. In order to give form to the vision, we needed to find a framework that somehow connected the seemingly disparate worlds of the Kichwa culture and modern business operating procedures. Although we looked everywhere for answers, little did we know that we'd find the guidance we sought brewing in the cauldron in front of us.

Step one, however, was to upgrade our living and working conditions in Quito from an existence based around youth hostels and Internet cafés. We rented a gorgeous two-story brick house for a whopping $600 a month that we could use as a home and an office. It was up on the top of the eastern side of the valley where Quito sits, right next to Parque Metropolitano, a huge city park with running and biking trails amid eucalyptus trees and a stunning view of the Pichincha volcano across the valley.

For reasons that are still beyond me, I thought getting a dog would be a great idea (as if I needed more to do), and fell in love with a rambunctious Husky puppy I named Noé (Noah in Spanish). My daily bliss in Quito became getting up around 5:00 a.m., guzzling a bunch of guayusa, and running a few miles with Noé in the cool Andean mist as the sun rose.

While $600 a month wasn't a ton in the U.S., it was more than we wanted to spend, so we rented out the extra rooms. Conviviality was also just our style. "La Casa Runa" quickly became home to a rotating cast of interns, expats, and Ecuadorian hipsters. At any one time, there were eight to ten people crashing there in bunk beds we crammed into the rooms. There was a friend who was working on an education program with the Secoya, another who was studying to be a lawyer with the goal of helping the indigenous people fight the oil companies, and a *quiteña* finishing law school. And then there was Scott, a sweet, hilarious, and totally jacked rugby player who was teaching English in Quito. It was Runa headquarters during the days and long nights, and a party zone on the weekends.

As the tasks we needed to address ballooned around us, we soon attracted a funky bunch of people to help. One day I looked around the office and took in the quirky but talented crew that had assembled around our mission. I'd met Nick Olson, our intern, at a bar when he stopped in Quito before taking part in a crazy motorcycle race from Lima to Buenos

Aires. He was so outgoing, friendly, and down to earth that I invited him to come back and intern with us when the race was finished, which he did. Nick was doing online research about tree transplanting procedures to see if there were any we could apply to guayusa.

On the other side of the room was Leo, one of our Kichwa interns, who was translating surveys from Spanish to Kichwa. He'd come to us via a 4:00 a.m. call from Alejandro, who said he wanted us to meet a young Kichwa university student who spoke perfect English. (Alejandro, of course, already had a vision that this student was going to be part of our team.) Given Alejandro's gift for exaggeration, I was dubious about the meaning of "perfect English," so when I called Leo, I spoke very slowly: "Hi, Leo. How . . . are . . . you?"

"Hey, what's up, dude?" Leo responded, sounding like he grew up in California. Startled, I wasn't sure if this meant he actually spoke fluent English, or if he'd just picked up this phrase from some traveling gringos. Playing it safe, I continued: "Oh, hey . . . dude. I'm good. What . . . are . . . you . . . doing?"

"I'm in finals now, just jamming like crazy," he replied effortlessly.

It turned out that, as a very precocious child, Leo had attached himself to American missionaries and just soaked up English. Leo, in short, was a character—both warmhearted and a total rabble-rouser, spiritually sensitive and adeptly metropolitan, hyperintelligent and undeniably hilarious.

Our strange posse definitely ruffled some feathers in the neighborhood, many of which belonged to our landlord, who was a very formal, older Ecuadorian gentleman not particularly fond of our 3:00 a.m. Frisbee games in the street.

Ancient Supply Chain Principles

To visit our various operating sites, several times a week I'd take the night bus between an alternating mix of Quito, Puyo, and Archidona. In the cool air of the Andean nights we would pass old plantations, cornfields, high mountain tundra, and snow-capped extinct volcanos before dipping down toward the Amazon, full of cattle, sugarcane, wild jungle and immense erosion from deforestation. The five hundred years since colonization were finely woven into the faces of both the landscape and the people, with beauty marks and scars that hinted at many generations of stories beneath the skin.

Despite my efforts to learn Ecuadorian cultural and geopolitical history, these bus rides made me acutely aware of how much of a foreigner I was in this place and how serious the potential implications of our work could be. I thought back to the Huichol practice of reflecting on how what we are doing today will impact generations far in the future. If we succeeded and guayusa became a hit in the U.S.—as we were sure it could be—we knew that down the road other people would start to export and sell it. As the first movers in the market, we were the ones designing the original terms not only for our own business but for the future industry at large.

This was an issue rife with historical color and shadow. The rubber boom of the early 1900s had been truly disastrous for the Amazonian people. Some tribes were totally wiped out. Others had to flee deep into the jungle to survive. Many indigenous people signed contracts with plantation masters for which they received material goods in return for labor. These "agreements" in effect enslaved them as their wages were never enough to pay off their debts: even death couldn't end the obligation; it only passed it on to the next generation. Contemporary accounts written in the early twentieth century tell a litany of horrors: indigenous workers were forced to work day and night, kept naked, whipped, dismembered, castrated, shot for fun, sold in the open market; women and children were raped; and on and on. The effects of this genocide are felt to this day.

Given the extreme sensitivity of this historical backdrop, we knew our good intentions were not enough: we needed careful planning.

In addition, there was the fact that we were building a business to produce and trade a living thing: guayusa. The Kichwa people were adamant that guayusa was an entity, a being, a "person" in its own way, with its own spirit and unique intelligence. They would even suggest that maybe we were not using guayusa for our purposes: rather, that the plant was exploiting *us* for its own ends.

You don't need to subscribe to the indigenous understanding of plant intelligence to see that there is at least an interesting thought exercise here. At the time, I read an incredible book by the British author Harry Hobhouse, *Seeds of Change: Six Plants That Transformed Mankind*, which details the history of cotton, tea, sugar, quinine, potatoes, and coca. He points out that none of these plants, for most of human history, were all that important to the vast majority of humans. Something happened with each that brought it out of obscurity to spread like wildfire throughout the world, bringing fundamental changes with them.

For example, quinine, a tonic made from the bark of the cinchona tree, was used for centuries by the indigenous people of Peru to treat high temperatures. In the 1700s, Europeans discovered it was also an effective treatment for malaria, which provided a golden key in foreigners' ability to colonize Africa and India. The desire for sugar led to the domination of the Caribbean and the beginning of the slave trade. Coca, used for centuries by South Americans for energy and hunger suppression, led to a massive criminal trade and large-scale incarceration when it was introduced in North America in the form of cocaine.

Many other plants have had world-changing impacts: the cultivation of wheat around 10,000 B.C. is what led humans to transform from hunter-gatherers to farmers; corn now drives the American system of industrial agriculture; coffee, introduced in Europe from Africa around 1700, became the fuel of the Industrial Revolution.

It's impossible to know when it's a plant's time, or the degree of impact it could have on the world. If we were going to bring guayusa to the world market, we would have to be ready for the full range of outcomes.

As for documentation about guayusa in recorded history, it basically didn't exist. After extensive research, we found only a few papers written about it and scant historical references.

Most intriguingly, the plant's origins are unknown. Guayusa has not been found to reproduce sexually in its native environment. A potential explanation of guayusa's sterility is that the plant could have been an ancient hybrid of other members of the *Ilex* genus—hybrids are often sterile—but there is no way to know definitively. One thing for certain is that every guayusa tree that exists today was planted by a person, and this reciprocal relationship between humans and guayusa stretches back thousands of years.

The earliest physical evidence of guayusa use is a bundle of the plant dating back to around A.D. 500, which was found in a shaman's tomb in the Bolivian Andes. Guayusa does not grow in Bolivia, so the find raised many questions: How did it get so far away? Was there a big guayusa trade at some point?

The first historical mentions of guayusa came in the late 1600s from missionaries working in the Amazon, who drank it to treat stomach pain. It also appears that Runa had a forerunner in a group of Jesuit priests who, in the mid-1700s, brought guayusa from their missions in the jungle to Quito with the intention of selling it. The dramatic difference was that they claimed guayusa to be a good treatment for venereal disease. Shockingly, that business never boomed, surely in part because guayusa does not actually treat venereal disease. (Indigenous people do say it reduces pain and inflammation, so perhaps the Jesuits stretched this claim.) For the next several centuries written accounts of guayusa appear only in occasional reports from missionaries and anthropologists venturing into the jungle.

As the first people trying to start a commercial guayusa operation in nearly three hundred years, we had a blank slate as far as establishing a supply chain. Starting from scratch, we were drawn by the business possibilities of being first to market, but more deeply by the opportunity to design the entire set of production and commercial standards for guayusa from the ground up. Who gets to do that?

Most agricultural products are dominated by low-quality, conventional production methods. Niche premium evolutions, like organic chocolate or Fair Trade coffee, arise over time, but these sustainable alternatives are just that: alternatives.

I'd worked a bit on some Fair Trade chocolate and coffee projects during my travels and studies and had seen what an immense challenge it is to shift such entrenched global industries. While Fair Trade chocolate is great, trying to nudge the entire eight hundred pound gorilla of the chocolate industry in a "fair" direction is a gargantuan task. The majority of the world's chocolate supply is produced on plantations in West Africa, where terrible working conditions and pay, and even the use of child labor, are the rule rather than the exception.

With guayusa, we had the opportunity to make certified organic and Fair Trade standards the norm, not the exception. We knew that these certifications were musts for us. We didn't care so much about slapping some shiny logos on our future packaging as an attempt at cause marketing, but because these were effective guidelines that reflected our values and could help us achieve the impact we were after.

Fair Trade would take care of the social and economic sides, guaranteeing that farmers we worked with would get a fair price for the guayusa and would have transparent and democratic organizations to represent them. Organic would ensure that we utilized environmentally sustainable practices to produce guayusa.

So we began researching what it would take to actually get certified, with no idea what we were in for.

Gathering Around the Fire

In the meantime, I spent more time in Napo and I got to more intimately know Virgilio's dad, Don Ernesto, who gave the impression of having an unbreakable core but a soft, welcoming shell. He had been gracious to us from the beginning, telling Dan and me that, like Gustavo in Pindo, he also had dreams about guayusa becoming popular across the world. That said, he had little to no interest in our ongoing "analysis" of either Kichwa myths or our business prospects. "*Demasiado pensar*" ("Too much thinking"), he always commented in his broken Spanish.

To me, "thinking through it" sounds like a principled approach to anything, but from a shamanic perspective it's not nearly enough. "Guayusa is about the heart and the soul," Don Ernesto said. "You have to develop a *relationship* with it and learn to listen. It already knows what to do. It will guide you."

In theory, the idea of building a supply chain from scratch sounded cool, innovative, and adventurous. But as we started to get our heads around the incredibly long list of questions we had to answer and the hoops to jump through to make it a reality, I don't think the word "overwhelmed" does justice to our feelings of terror, confusion, and shortness of breath.

Moreover, the concept I'd relished at Brown of building bridges and connecting cultures with business as a type of modern poetry *sounded* cool, but I started to struggle with the actual grind of it. In the jungle I loved getting up and drinking guayusa, learning Kichwa words, hearing rich myths weave in and out of each other, and feeling the forest vibrate and rouse at sunrise. But as our business began to take root, my day-to-day was increasingly consumed by meetings with lawyers and bureaucrats, researching FDA import requirements, grappling with Ecuadorian export laws, preparing excel spreadsheets, reviewing agreements . . . and on and on.

I noticed that I was letting the pressures of business reality dominate my attention and attitude, and failing to engage the shamanic tools I had learned in Peru. I felt like we were *thinking* so much, struggling to cram this ineffable plant into this high-growth business mind-set, without the trust, without the space for guayusa itself, and without relying on the central element of guayusa from the Kichwa point of view: a real, living relationship with it.

In an effort to reorient myself, I spent a few days with Virgilio and Don Ernesto in their community. Virgilio and I would get up at 3:00 a.m., jump in the cold river to wake up, and then drink guayusa with his family. As the sun began to rise, I'd sneak off in the jungle to get some moments by myself. Taking the time to sit silently with a cup of guayusa held to my heart, I would "talk" to it. (And, yes, my conscious mind constantly yelled, *You're crazy! You're weird! This means nothing!*)

Despite my mind's protests, I pressed ahead, saying: "Hi, Guayusa Spirit, whoever, whatever, if ever you are. I humbly ask for your help to guide me in sharing you with the world in a good way. Please guide my thoughts, visions, work, and ideas today. Thank you for your light and support." Then I would give a small handful of tobacco to a plant or tree nearby as homage to something greater.

Something began to happen after doing this ritual and connecting to guayusa. Rather than "thinking" through opportunities, challenges, or what I had to do that day, it was like a change in channel to another kind of thinking or knowing. The tone of this process lacked the feeling of grasping, struggle, and uncertainty, and felt almost as if nudged from beyond. I think Don Ernesto would say this was guayusa teaching and guiding me, a concept I felt more and more open to; but I also wondered if mixing an attitude of openness and humility with the experience of drinking guayusa just helped my brain organize my thoughts better.

This new openness helped me intuit a place where the separate realities of our business interests and indigenous inspiration could meet.

As a company just being born, we found ourselves at that transition point between the dream world and the waking world, which is exactly when the Kichwa communities drink guayusa. The guayusa ceremony gathers people around the fire to share their dreams and weave them into a larger, collective story. What if our role was just expanding the guayusa ceremony? What if we built a business *like* a guayusa ceremony?

It was essentially the seed of friendship and collaboration that brought Dan, Charlie, Laura, Aden, and me together in the first place; even the venture capitalist we pitched to during our final presentation at Brown unexpectedly commented on the camaraderie between us. What if, beyond a research strategy, our actual business also gathered people around the metaphorical fire of our intention, got everyone to talk about their dreams and ideas for what this could be, and then collectively wove them together?

Hanging out in Virgilio's community, I began to acutely understand that the decision to collaborate or not collaborate really doesn't exist for his people. The traditional indigenous village is largely pre-institutional: the people sitting around the fire drinking guayusa really are each other's sole support. They are the judicial system, health care system, bank, insurance agency, education system, etc. If you need help putting a roof on your hut, it's the people in that circle who help. If you need a loan, it has to come from someone there. If you're sick, it's the shaman who provides health care. Everything has to come from someone within the collective.

Any start-up, let alone a shamanically oriented one, is essentially similar. As fledgling entrepreneurs, we also had no access to institutions—no lines of credit, no shareholders, no health care—just people willing to contribute to what we were doing. It made sense to invite them into our circle to share their ideas and help us "interpret" the dream of our company as it became a reality.

Intentional Friction

Dan and I spent more and more time discussing ways we could integrate this collaborative approach into the core structure of our business. We knew from the start we were going to have to set up at least two entities: one in Ecuador to produce guayusa, and another in the United States to package and sell it. At first we wanted the Ecuadorian side to be nonprofit, which we thought would keep us focused on the mission to help farmers, enable us to get grants, and generally make our interactions with communities and the government more amicable by removing the profit motive.

We learned, however, that there were some problems with that idea. For one, Ecuadorian law basically forbids nonprofits from buying, selling, and exporting products. And even if that had not been the case, after speaking with the Kichwa communities, we realized that there had been so many failed nonprofit schemes before us that the term carried negative connotations.

People viewed nonprofits as wishy-washy, do-gooder operations that accomplished little. So from the beginning we found it necessary to emphasize that we were a business and our purpose was to make money for everyone involved. Early on, people would refer to us by default as "El Proyecto de Guayusa" ("the Guayusa Project"), but we had to continually emphasize that this wasn't some short-term project: we were building a business and an industry for the long term.

Of course, we worried that if we were only a business, that would mean taking on investors who would rightly expect to see a return on their investment, and our social mission could get overshadowed. We had heard about "hybrid organizations" that combine both for-profit and nonprofit organizations, and had some intuitive sense that creating a hybrid structure would best support our mission. We had only vague ideas about what our nonprofit side would actually do differently from our for-profit side, but we had a bit of a blind faith that it would sort itself out over time.

An intentional aspect of the design was to *purposely* create the potential for friction between the two sides; in other words, if everything worked right, we expected the for-profit and nonprofit sides to occasionally clash in healthy ways. For example, part of the nonprofit foundation's work in Ecuador is to help train the farmers and strengthen their local cooperatives. We realized "empowering the farmers" meant that the nonprofit could get involved in helping them negotiate higher prices for guayusa, even if that created a headache for the company. We felt we had to do this to make sure Runa remained true to its social mission in the long term. Since friction and disagreement would be there one way or another, we felt like inviting it into the business would be healthier than letting it fester under the surface.

So we went ahead and established four separate entities: a business in Ecuador to produce guayusa; a business in the U.S. to package, bottle, and sell guayusa; a foundation in Ecuador; and another foundation in the U.S. Dan and I became the board and the management of all of these entities. Not too long ago, neither of us had a job. Now we each had four of them!

Practical Shape-Shifting

Unfortunately, we burned through the $70,000 we'd won in the business plan competitions at a shocking rate and soon were back to running on fumes. A low point came when I went to the jungle town of Macas to visit a peanut-growing cooperative and had to get back to Quito for a meeting. I got dropped off at the town's tiny airport but I felt a knot in my stomach as I walked inside and saw a window outside the security point: to use the airport, you had to pay the municipality a $10 departure tax. I had absolutely no money on me.

Our credit cards were maxed out and our bank account dry. Without planning ahead for the tax, I couldn't pay it, and there was no way I was leaving without coughing up the fee. I finally went into the parking lot and sold my headphones to a teenager, who gave me just enough to get me out of town.

I had to get on that plane, since the meeting we had in Quito was very important. Working through the contacts we got from Yolanda Kakabadse, we'd made a connection with the Ecuadorian export ministry, which was offering a $50,000 grant to a company selling an Ecuadorian-made product abroad. We had applied, and I rushed to a meeting at an office building in Quito's commercial district, where I met Dan. We ended up across a conference table from the four export ministry employees who were evaluating our proposal.

One essential skill Dan and I quickly learned was the ability to tell a compelling story. More accurately, we had to develop a variety of compelling stories about what we envisioned for Runa. We became adept at this form of "shape-shifting."

In shamanism, shape-shifting is a common idea: during ceremonies people often have fantastical visions in which they see themselves as a puma or transforming into a snake. Much to my own frustration at the time, I never managed to access anything that cool. I did, however, develop an appreciation for more practical dimensions of what I interpreted shape-shifting to be.

I learned that even though you may have one big, overarching narrative as an organization, it can always be broken down into many smaller pieces. With Runa, we tailored our story for our audience: what we said was always true, but the emphasis and focal point shifted. So, with businesspeople, we talked about the functional properties of guayusa and the potential market for it in the U.S. With the Kichwa communities, we spoke about how it could be a bridge to share something incredibly valuable from their culture with the world and make a living doing it. With environmental groups, we spoke about how guayusa offered people in the jungle a sustainable way to earn money and conserve the rainforest.

We knew from reading the goals that the export ministry had published that they really wanted to promote nontraditional exports to diversify their economy away from oil.

"Ecuador has great chocolate," I said, "but a lot of other countries also have chocolate. No one else has guayusa. Guayusa can be *the* emblematic Ecuadorian export."

I was making this up on the spot, but Dan nodded as if he'd heard it a thousand times before.

We told them about the market for energy drinks in the U.S. and how guayusa was primed to explode, creating a huge opportunity for Ecuadorian farmers.

We promised that if we got the grant, it would go toward buying a drying chamber and establishing "the world's first research and development center for guayusa," painting a picture that made it resemble something like a NASA lab. In reality, we were planning on setting it up in Oscar's garage in Archidona.

Two months later I received a call while at "La Casa Runa" saying that our application had been approved! We were so ecstatic that we blasted some Diplo dance tracks and darted around the office, jumping up on the couches and shaking like overexcited puppies. Surprisingly, the export ministry wanted to give the grant to our company in Ecuador, rather than awarding it to the Runa Foundation, our nonprofit. Rather than supporting a nonprofit that would constantly need new donations, they felt more comfortable providing targeted support to help build a business that would be self-sustaining over time. Honestly, we didn't care which organization the funds went to. Free money was free money.

We arranged to buy a drying chamber in Quito and planned to ship it down to Archidona, when we discovered one big problem: in the line-by-line budget we'd included in the application, we'd forgotten to allocate any money for transporting the dryer from Quito to the jungle! Every single penny had already been designated, it was impossible to go back and ask for more, and we had very little additional cash on hand.

Dan and I pondered it before mutually agreeing that we had only one option: El Limón. A battered old pickup truck that we'd bought for $900, El Limón ("the Lemon") was our old, belligerent ox for carting supplies and people around our various work sites. Loading it with an industrial dryer the size of an extra-large refrigerator and heading down a mountain was something we hadn't tried.

It took eight guys to lift the drying chamber into the bed of the pickup, which sank under the weight, the back end tilting down toward the pavement. I had to stick around Quito for a handful of meetings, so Dan climbed in with Noé the Husky riding shotgun. As he pulled out, El Limón's engine moaned and whined.

In the book *The Hard Thing About Hard Things: Building a Business When There Are No Easy Answers* (probably the only business book I read early on that felt like it actually taught me how to run a business; I highly recommend it), the Silicon Valley venture capitalist Ben Horowitz writes that, as an entrepreneur, you have to believe in calculus, not statistics. In other words, you must have complete conviction that there is an answer for everything, that you will find it, and that no matter what, things are going to work. Without that certitude, the challenges will be too big and you will just be overwhelmed.

Dan certainly had that attitude. The trip from Quito to Archidona, which normally takes around four hours, includes an elevation drop of 7,500 feet. As Dan headed down, he found that the extra weight was too much for El Limón's brakes, which began to smoke and stop working. When he pulled over and looked under the wheel wells, he saw the disc brakes were glowing red. He waited for them to cool down and drove a little farther, until they starting smoking again.

He repeated this ritual until he got to Archidona eighteen hours later. Starting, nearly overheating, stopping, waiting, starting again. Patience, patience, and more patience. If there was ever a metaphor for founding a business in the middle of the Amazon, this is it.

Chapter 6

Negotiate Your Boundaries

After burning all our assumptions about traditional business, nonprofits, and organizational structures, Dan and I now needed to design an organization that served our unique goals. Managing the boundaries of that container and selecting who and what we wanted inside this space would constantly challenge us throughout our subsequent growth. Given that our core philosophy and growth strategy was to be highly collaborative and open, the very idea of boundaries was a tough one to reconcile. We learned on the job.

Oscar's garage, which was on a side street in Archidona, had bamboo walls and a corrugated, patchy tin roof; "hermetically sealed" would not have described the container in which our first research and production facility would develop. With his chickens running around everywhere, you even had to be careful where you stepped.

The Kichwa communities had no formalized way of making guayusa. Traditionally, as we'd seen, they'd made it by boiling whole leaves in a large pot for anywhere between thirty minutes and seven hours. (Because guayusa leaves do not have any tannins as other teas do, it can be brewed for long periods of time without becoming astringent.) That meant the flavor of a cup of guayusa could range all the way from light and vegetal, similar to green tea, to a strong, dark, and earthy brew with hints of mesquite and molasses.

When we earnestly asked different communities what they considered to be the "classic" guayusa flavor, the ultimate answer was "somewhere in the middle"—not too green but maintaining a brightness of flavor, and not too dark but harnessing the plant's richer earthy notes.

With that as our guidance, we set to work on figuring out how to "industrially" dry the leaves to achieve these characteristics and come up with a uniform product. We intently researched processing methods for green tea, black tea, and yerba maté to get ideas, and then just started messing around. Piles of leaves on plastic tarps on the garage floor were shuffled onto large metal trays in the big steel box that was the drying chamber, and then we fired that sucker up!

Strictly speaking, I should mention that guayusa is not technically a "tea." Having been much more of an herbal tea drinker, I didn't realize that green tea, black tea, white tea, oolong tea, and pu-erh tea all come from the same plant (botanical name *Camellia sinensis*). To professionals in the tea trade, *only* derivatives of the *Camellia sinensis* plant can *rightfully* (best read with an English accent) be called "teas." So one *shan't* (again, best read with an English accent) use the word tea to refer to infusions like mint or chamomile, but should call them by the French word "tisane." (For the record, I personally still say mint tea, hibiscus tea, and guayusa tea. Dried leaves or flowers + hot water equals tea in my book.)

But whatever name you wanted to use, we had to create a consistent, standardized drink we would bring to market, and that raised a lot of questions.

For starters, which leaves do you choose to dry in the first place? For all types of *Camellia sinensis* tea, you always harvest and use "two leaves and a bud." In other words, just the youngest two leaves and the sprout at the very end of each branch. With guayusa, it was just the opposite. Farmers harvest the mature leaves, which, being from the holly family, are quite thick and large. (Guayusa leaves can be longer than the length of your hand.) We decided to stick with the traditional practice of harvesting mature leaves (as is the custom with yerba maté as well).

On the drying side, we learned that most industrial black tea is produced using the CTC (cut, tear, and curl) method, in which leaves are fed into cylindrical rollers lined with hundreds of metal teeth that rapidly crush, tear, and curl the leaves. The resulting pellets are then run through high-speed air chambers that dry them in as little as fifteen minutes. Some of the largest factories in the world can process over 50 million pounds of fresh tea leaves per year! The vast majority of the world's tea is made this way, and the result is an inexpensive, bold, and quick-brewing drink (think your average cup of Lipton). Expensive machinery, low quality, and high volume requirements were exactly what we *didn't* want, so another option was scratched off the list.

We thought that looking at yerba maté production would be more instructive, since it is also a type of holly leaf and a botanical cousin of guayusa. (Their botanical names are *Ilex paraguariensis* and *Ilex guayusa*.) Yerba maté is native to the Atlantic rainforest in Argentina and Brazil and was traditionally brewed into tea by the native Guaraní and Tupí communities there. Beloved in countries such as Argentina, Brazil, Uruguay, Bolivia, and Chile, it has also become relatively popular among natural foods consumers in the U.S. over the last two decades.

We learned that when yerba maté is harvested, the branches are often dried by a wood fire, which imparts a smoky flavor, and then aged for months or even years. We had neither the interest nor the time to try this with guayusa, so another dead end.

The most relevant processing system we found was in the more artisanal methods of making green or oolong tea, in which fresh-picked leaves are spread out for several hours so they begin to wilt and then get "rolled" so that their cell walls start to break down. That begins the process of oxidation, which can last anywhere from a few hours to several days, depending on the type of tea you're making. Some teas are even rolled and oxidized several times.

Oxidation, or "withering," we discovered, was the absolute key. Ultimately all that differentiates green tea from black tea is the degree of withering. Oxidation is what happens when you cut an apple and it turns brown, or when leaves change color in the fall. Very complicated chemical reactions happen during this fragile limbo state of withering, transforming flavorless compounds into flavorful ones, for better or worse. To get it right demands close care and attention. Certain tea masters in Asia will even sleep next to their withering leaves, smelling and tasting them every hour, to trace and sculpt the exact evolution of their flavor.

For guayusa, we had to experiment with the amount of time the leaves spent between harvest and drying, the amount of leaves on each drying tray, temperatures, times, etc., etc., to get this process right. Some batches tasted like broccoli, others like tar with hints of rotting black pepper. Oscar had a friend who ran a bar up the road and was a total night owl, so we got him to come check on batches of leaves drying at night on occasion. When we found him passed out on the floor in a pile of leaves one morning at 6:00 a.m., we realized there are limitations to the "Hey I know a guy" approach . . .

After months of playing around, we started to get some workable product. We fed it into an electric grinder we'd picked up in Quito, exactly the same kind of machine a butcher uses to grind beef. The result wasn't uniform in shape or size, but it resembled something that approximated tea you might actually feel safe consuming, which was very exciting at the time.

As we had long planned, Dan then returned to Providence to get started on brand and product development. He joined Charlie, who had been helping us while still in his last semester of school.

Starting to get some guayusa to Dan and Charlie from Ecuador to the U.S. proved to be yet another challenge. We didn't have an export license at this point and simply mailing packages of chopped-up green plant material through the regular mail from South America to the United States presented some obvious issues.

We found there was a courier service in Quito that, through some strange backdoor legislation, had a setup where you could send a package weighing less than two kilograms to the United States without an export certificate. It was OK as long as it was going to one of their offices in the U.S. The closest one we found to Providence was about an hour away, in Old Saybrook, Connecticut.

We arranged it so that every few weeks Oscar put some dried guayusa on the bus from Archidona to Quito. Someone from our office picked it up at the bus terminal at the southern end of the city, and we packaged it into 1.9-kilogram Ziploc bags covered in duct tape, which ended up shaped like deformed footballs. I once tried roping about eight of these to the back of my friend's motorcycle to take to the courier, and not surprisingly, one of the packages slipped when I hit a pothole, fell onto the wheel of the motorcycle, and erupted in a bright green guayusa cloud behind me.

Yet another quirk was that the courier had to tape a copy of the sender's ID onto each package. My passport picture was taken when I was seventeen, back when my hair was down to my shoulders. I remember being in a spunky mood the day I got my picture taken and offered up a wide-eyed, head-cocked, surly smile to the camera. As a result, I appeared to be a cross between Mike Myers in *Wayne's World* and the drummer from Metallica. By the grace of guayusa, that picture slapped on eight different duct-taped 1.9-kilo footballs of Amazonian leaves somehow never aroused any suspicion with customs. Like the vines that twist, loop, and squeeze their way up to the sky through the thick jungle, we were finding our way where we saw the glimpses of light.

If Your Business Doesn't Work, Your Mission Means Nothing

Not everything was well in our supply chain, however. From the very beginning, our operations in Napo had gone better than those in Pastaza. One reason was simply that the soil in Napo was better than in Pastaza, so they had an easier time growing guayusa. Another was that outside development had started much more recently in Pastaza, with rapid exploitation of the jungle as well as oil drilling. That created a harsher edge in the city of Puyo and a distrustful sentiment in the communities surrounding it.

In comparison, Archidona, the main city in Napo, was founded in the mid-sixteenth century and had a much longer history with the outside world. Given its slower process of exposure, the exploitation of the jungle was not nearly as intense and the people and atmosphere were a lot more chilled out.

Beyond that, our problems in Pastaza went deeper still.

Alejandro had introduced us to Luis Yumbo, whom we hired to run our Pastaza operation. Luis, who was around sixty, was charismatic, charming, and funny. A longtime politician and former state senator, he'd played a leadership role in many of the indigenous uprisings of the 1980s and 1990s and had just finished a stint as the vice president of the indigenous federation representing all the Amazonian tribes in Ecuador. We were excited that he wanted to work with us and thought his connections would be super-helpful, so we really didn't do any additional due diligence when we hired him.

Setting up our drying chamber in Oscar's garage really—

there is no other way to put this—pissed off Luis. He felt we were favoring Napo over Pastaza.

We had been looking for months for land where we could establish our main Runa headquarters and factory once we got the funding. A few weeks after we set up the garage operation, Luis came to me and said he'd found some land in Fátima, just north of Puyo in Pastaza, that we could have for free. At this stage of our growth, "for free" were two of the magical words we lived by, so Luis had my full attention.

The property was about twenty acres and came with a tangled history. About a decade prior, the government had given the land to the regional indigenous federation to start an animal rescue center and endangered animal breeding operation. The plan was to raise animals such as agoutis, which are large jungle rodents that the Kichwa people love to hunt and eat. Like the vast majority of similar projects, it bombed, although there were still some run-down buildings on the site as well as a few animals, including a friendly tapir (a relative of the rhinoceros that looks like an enormous anteater). We named her Bambi.

Luis made it seem like the land still belonged to the indigenous federation, and we even received a formal-looking letter from the president of the federation granting us use while we worked on the title transfer. From the start, Dan was more suspicious than I was. "So, we're taking over a zoo?" was his simple, telling question to me when I first told him about it.

I was, as usual, overly optimistic about the situation, and desperate to boot. If we were going to raise real outside capital, I felt like the story and romance wasn't enough. We needed a "legitimate" operation—you know, operating permits, an export license, no chickens in our factory—and I was willing to "get creative" to make that happen.

We invested a substantial amount of our meager funds into building our first legit tree nursery and fixing up one of the buildings, where we moved our furniture, equipment, and intern housing set-up over. In the meantime I kept asking Luis about getting the title to the land, to which he always answered with "*Ya mismo.*" The literal translation would be "Right now," but in Ecuador, I came to see that the meaning is quite a bit murkier. It could be "I'm right around the corner; be there in thirty seconds." More often, it indicates something like "I need to eat lunch, go back to the other side of town, run some errands, and then I'll be there in three hours."

After several months of this I was becoming very nervous. It didn't get better when Luis tried to reassure me by telling me that even without the title there was nothing to worry about: If the government ever tried to evict us, we could get five hundred people to come with guns and machetes to scare them off, and then squat on the land until they gave us the title. I told him that, as a business, getting people to squat at our headquarters in order to keep the government from claiming it couldn't be our plan!

Our mission as a social enterprise was to work with the indigenous farmers as partners for the good of everyone, and here we were running into major problems with a longstanding member of the local indigenous leadership whom we had embedded in a critical role at Runa. My stomach sank every time I thought about the land deal falling through. Luis also had a way of making it seem like my questions about the title of the land somehow reflected a lack of trust in him personally, in our team, in our mission, and even in the spirit of guayusa itself.

Adding to the urgency of the problem: despite our endless attempts to bring in more funding, a few close leads fell through at the last minute, and carrying the cost of operations in two provinces began to look untenable.

Dan had befriended Rich Matusow, one of the earliest employees and the original vice president of sales for Sambazon, the leading açaí berry company in the U.S., which sustainably sourced from Brazil. On a relatively desperate call with Rich he respectfully but forcefully repeated one clear point to us: "If the business doesn't fundamentally work, your mission means absolutely nothing," he said. "You need to make smart *business* decisions in service of the mission and ensure that your whole company doesn't implode. If your business is not successful, you won't be helping anyone."

So we finally chose to pull the plug in Pastaza. I broke the news to Luis during a meeting at an ice cream shop in Puyo. He was obviously disappointed and tried to change my mind, telling me that everything was going to be fine. As he began to understand that I wasn't negotiating with him, his tone became more enigmatic. "You *really* need to think about this," he said ominously before walking away.

Considering that Luis and his friends had told us stories about revolutionaries burning down buildings and threatening foreigners with rifles—not to mention marching to Quito and literally overthrowing the national government in 2000—I was scared.

Nevertheless, we found a new location for our office in Archidona with room in the back to build our first small-scale factory, just up the street from Oscar's garage. The six-bedroom house on a quarter acre cost us all of $250 a month in rent. We didn't own it, it wouldn't be permanent, but I made myself comfortable with the half step.

We still needed to retrieve our equipment from the property in Fátima, and I thought we could avoid a confrontation by going to get it in the middle of the night. With a few of our field staff from Napo and two interns, we borrowed a large truck from one of Oscar's friends and pulled in around 11:00 p.m.

About ninety minutes later we were just about to grab the last desk and put it in the truck when four pickup trucks rolled up and blocked us in. Luis stepped out with twelve other men he had brought as muscle.

"What are you doing in *our* place, Tyler?" he asked.

It was very odd. For my whole time in Ecuador up to that point, no one in the jungle had ever pronounced "Tyler" correctly. Maybe I was just freaked out and hearing things, but I swore Luis had just said it perfectly.

"Luis, you know we're shutting down in Pastaza," I said. "We've come to get our stuff."

He wasn't going for that. The next four hours devolved into a screaming match inside one of the decrepit buildings.

"You gringo traitor!" Luis yelled. "You are trying to steal our stuff, trying to steal our traditions! You're losing faith because you have no spine! How dare you turn your back on us and turn your back on the farmers?"

"Luis," I shouted back, feeling tingles on my neck and trying to control my legs from shaking, "I invested twenty thousand dollars here just on your word! You promised me the title months ago. We're just squatting on this freaking animal farm!"

It went on and on until it gradually shifted into an attempted negotiation. "How about you pay for us to get another office in town for another three months and go from there?" Luis asked.

Labor laws in Ecuador require a company to give fired employees hefty termination fees, so as it was Runa had to pay Luis around $1,000 and his assistant director, Byron, another $600. That amount of cash goes a long way in Ecuador. I suggested to Luis that he use that money if he wanted to keep the office open.

Luis backed off a little. "Well, I mean, you know, that money is for, well, it's for us, it's for our personal expenses," he said, breaking from his usually assured tone.

I lost it and kicked a table over. "That! That right there, Luis, is your true color. That is where you are and where you want to be, a supposed leader who won't put your money where your mouth is, who won't stand up for your very own people, but who will try to bully the gringo into doing it for you. I won't have any more of this. I'm done."

Fuming, I turned and marched to the door that his goons were blocking. Luis said nothing and they stepped aside, allowing our group to leave.

We made it back to Archidona with our equipment as the sun was rising. No one spoke as we sat on the steps of our new office, drinking guayusa. Finally, Patricio, one of the field staff, pulled out a pouch of jungle tobacco. "Tyler," he said, "during that whole time I was calling on the spirits of my ancestors to help you."

He rolled a few *mapacho* cigarettes and handed them around the group. We smoked in silence, passed gourds of guayusa, and prepared ourselves for another day of work.

Leaders, Managers, and Entrepreneurs

Thankful for the successful though unsettling escape from Pastaza, in short order we found ourselves with leadership issues in Napo as well. As our operations consolidated there, I became more demanding and hands-on, and started asking Oscar for weekly reports and clear monthly goals. We were managing a grant budget, and we needed to take steps to streamline operations and move past the scrappy attitude that had gotten us to that point, but Oscar did not take well to the new responsibilities.

It was tough, because in the very early days Oscar had been great at working by the seat of his pants and getting things done. If you needed a nursery designed, he could sketch one on the back of a napkin and get it built in a week. If you had to find obscure tools in the jungle, he could do it. He was perfect for a new operation in which there weren't defined roles or much of a hierarchy. He was diligent, resourceful, hardworking, caring, and smart. Sadly, leading a team and managing people weren't exactly in his wheelhouse.

My dad, through his work in real estate, had introduced me to the concept of the architect's triangle. Its three points are speed, cost, and quality. He told me that when you want a building done, you can have any two, but you'll lose the third. Want something cheap and quick? Quality will suck. Want something high-quality on a tight deadline? Gonna cost ya.

I've come to think there is a similar triangle for business executives, but the points are entrepreneur, leader, and manager. However, you rarely get even two of the three: each skill set is essentially very different, although in modern business-speak they seem to get quite confused and dangerously interchanged.

Being entrepreneurial is about being resourceful, finding creative solutions, thinking on your feet, and being flexible in the face of immense pressure. Leadership is an entirely different thing: establishing a vision; inspiring others to follow and execute; making big, important decisions; upholding core values. Then there's management: precisely executing a plan; attention to detail; an eye for efficiency and optimization; diligently following processes.

People who are strong entrepreneurs are sometimes good leaders but not often great managers. Superb managers are usually not natural entrepreneurs. In my experience it is the rare unicorn who combines all three qualities.

Whereas Luis had been a strong leader, a passable manager, and a mediocre entrepreneur, Oscar, it was clear, was a strong entrepreneur, decent with leadership, and not into management at all. The more we needed him to focus and execute the plan, the more he started to drop the ball. He wasn't getting in his reports on a timely basis, and our field staff seemed to be marching to the beat of their own drum. For months I tried everything I could think of—spending three hours at the end of every week reviewing reports and sitting there while he prepared plans for the following week, giving him management books, getting him to attend workshops in Quito—but little changed.

When he missed the deadline to submit the first status report to the export ministry for our project, it delayed the next disbursement of funding we desperately needed. The disappointment on everyone's face when I announced to our team on a Friday afternoon that we would not be getting the money we required to fund the next two weeks' activities is something I'll never forget. No one wanted an unexpected "vacation." I had to let Oscar go.

It left us in a pinch, as I had no one ready to take over his position as regional manager. Drinking guayusa early one morning behind the office, I contemplated my sparse options. I could try to run the team myself, but I was already stretched thin, wasn't even in Napo full-time, and needed to get back to the U.S. as soon as possible to work with Dan. I could promote one of the field staff, but none of them had management experience. We could try recruiting someone else in Napo, but the executive leadership pool was tiny and the recruiting process could take forever. I also feared another situation like the one we had suffered in Pastaza. As I polished off another large gourd of guayusa and the first rays of sunlight started to appear and the first buses rolled by, a whacky idea popped in my head.

Nick Olson, our former intern, had returned to Colorado but was already on his way back to Ecuador to run our intern program. Once he arrived, our conversation began something like "Hey, Nick, so you know how you thought you were coming back here to manage interns . . . Well, how about you manage the whole operation in Napo instead?"

It was a stretch, yes, and his initial reaction was certainly not favorable. I tried explaining to him the reasons I wanted him in that role: we had great communication, I trusted him, he was hyper-diligent, and everybody respected the way he handled himself, setting a great tone for the next phase of the organization. After a few days of discussions and Nick making sure that my expectations weren't too high, he accepted (more like acquiesced, I suppose).

Nick quickly learned about some of the job's complications.

During his first week he had to make an emergency trip to a remote community to repair relations after a botched sale. The community had recently harvested guayusa to sell to us, but the bridge on the way there washed out. By the time our truck arrived, three days late, the harvested leaves had all rotted, leaving the villagers with nothing to sell and no income for their hard work. Nick and our new factory manager, Manolo, had to try and smooth things over.

Upon arrival, Nick greeted them with his usual huge smile and "Howdy! Life is great!" attitude. Unimpressed, they simply escorted him and Manolo to the main community meeting room, where everyone was gathered. As soon as they were in, the door was locked behind them.

A few of the old Kichwa grandmothers sat next to a big mound of jungle stinging nettles and a basket full of hot peppers. Yelling in Kichwa, running around and waving their fists at him, it didn't take any linguistic skills for Nick to know that their intention was to whip him with nettles and squirt burning hot pepper juice in his eyes (traditional Kichwa punishment rituals).

Somehow, in typical Nick fashion, he explained the situation in a very sincere and heartfelt way, offered to pay 50 percent for the rotten leaves, committed to another harvest the following week, and then proposed certain protocols to get the harvest over the river if the bridge washed out again in the future. The leaders appreciated the thoughtfulness, sincerity, and clear planning, and agreed to the terms. Then Nick managed to get everyone laughing again.

It turned out, oddly enough, that Nick ended up as a neutral party in the thorny tangle of Ecuadorian racial politics.

Oscar was a mestizo, and, due to the colonial history, there has always been tension between mestizos and the indigenous communities, something Oscar had to deal with when working with farmers. As an energetic young, white American, Nick, like Dan and me, fell outside this specific social divide. The indigenous farmers took to him and he made up for his lack of experience with an incredible ability to listen and make people feel respected. As a manager, he was hyper-focused on translating the needs from the field back to headquarters and vice versa, being meticulous and thorough—just what we needed.

And while Nick's job was far from a walk in the park (there are many more vipers in Napo than your average park), Cass, the brilliant, affable young British woman we hired in his place to run the internship program, eventually became his wife, so it all worked out just fine for him.

With the basics of our supply chain up and running, it was time for me to get ready to move back to the U.S. to help grow the domestic side of the business that Dan had begun to lay the foundation for. Although Nick was leading the operation in Napo, I most urgently needed to bring someone on who could run the entire business in Ecuador.

Having made a complete mess of our Ecuadorian incorporation papers, our early accounting, our team's employment contracts, and just about everything in between, we realized we needed someone with just two abilities. First, they needed to know how to run a company in Ecuador. Second, they had to have the patience to deal with us.

We put out the word about our need for a general manager, and the first person we received a résumé from was Francisco Mantilla. He was nothing short of a gift from above. I met with him and knew within five minutes that he was our guy: he'd not only run part of the Ministry of the Environment and worked as a professional export manager, he had lived in the U.S., worked for a U.S. supermarket chain, tried being an entrepreneur himself, and spoke fluent English. I sent him an offer letter the next day, and he's been a critical part of Runa for the last seven years, growing to become CEO of Runa for all of Latin America. Francisco is that rare mix of phenomenal manager, top-notch entrepreneur, and firm leader.

Refusing to give into our super-casual style, he came over to the house in Quito every day at 6:00 a.m. looking ready for court: suit, tie, hair neatly styled. His cordial demeanor encased an extremely savvy business intellect and shrewd eye. The combination of these features gave him the ability to negotiate the pants off people.

One of the many issues he was tasked with was smoothing our relationship with our landlord in Quito, who was growing less and less tolerant of our insanity.

One afternoon he came over fuming about us forgetting to take out the trash, my dog pooping on his lawn and eating his tulips, people coming in and out at all hours of the night—the list went on.

"Is this a business or some sort of gringo party house?" he yelled at Francisco.

In his calm Jedi manner, Francisco replied, "Sir, I can assure you, this is a very serious business operation. We are working tirelessly to support the indigenous communities of our country."

The landlord sighed, smiled, and told Francisco that he appreciated having such a respectable *quiteño* around he could relate to.

At that moment, our roommate Scott came up the stairs, his burly rugby-player frame on display, since he was totally naked except his tighty-whities. With his terrible Spanish accent, he cheerfully said "*¡Hola!*" to the owner, gave a general's salute, and strutted into the kitchen. It was about 2:00 p.m. on a Tuesday. I can't say Francisco was as successful at calming down the owner after that.

Refining the Mission and Getting Certified

While Francisco took the reins of the for-profit side, we needed someone who could run Runa Foundation and make it into its own organization. Up to that point Runa Foundation existed as a nascent vision and not much more than a set of incorporation papers.

Through a long chain of conversations and introductions we were introduced to Eliot Logan-Hines, a native of Austin, Texas, who was finishing his master's degree from the Yale School of Forestry & Environmental Studies. Eliot had spent the prior decade working on agroforestry and conservation initiatives in Latin America.

On a fundraising trip through the Bay Area, Dan and I met Eliot at a coffee shop in East Oakland where we talked for a few hours about financing mechanisms for carbon sequestration programs, squatters on his farm in Costa Rica, and challenges with Fair Trade coffee supply chains. Eliot was clearly brilliant, opinionated, and just a strange breed of human being. He had this nutty professor–spritely wizard nature to him that was unlike anyone I'd ever met, and his life sounded straight out of a Gabriel García Márquez novel, full of odd circumstances, bizarre characters, and weird twists. It was immediately clear that his breadth of experience enabled him to view difficult issues at odd angles and come up with creative solutions.

Eliot later told us that after that first meeting he was blown away by the potential for guayusa and the Runa business—so blown away that his immediate thought was *How I can steal this idea and do it better than these schmucks?* Unaware of his characteristically mischievous intentions, we wanted to test the waters and build a relationship with Eliot, so we offered him a consulting contract to assess the viability of our agroforestry model and carbon credit programs.

His work was stellar and, beyond the confines of the specific project, he challenged us to think about long-term impact, our hybrid organizational structure, and the potential conservation impacts of guayusa production in entirely new ways. As our relationship developed, he helped us create an eight-word mission statement to frame the future impact of Runa's work.

We'd learned about eight-word mission statements from the Mulago Foundation, which is dedicated to assisting social enterprises that address the needs of the very poor. Kevin Starr, the managing director, and Laura Hattendorf, the head of investments, had stressed to us that mushy words such as "empowerment," "capacity building," and "sustainability" mean nothing. A mission statement should say exactly what you're trying to accomplish with a verb, a target population, and an outcome that implies something to measure—in eight words or less. "Save kids' lives in Uganda" or "Rehabilitate coral reefs in the Western Pacific" were two examples they gave.

We wanted our work to prove the value of the Amazon in

concrete, tangible ways and to help shift the broader conversation away from moralistic concepts of "needing to save the native peoples" or more distant goals about maintaining global oxygen production and carbon sequestration. With economics as our fighting ground, we wanted to prove that it is more *profitable* for farmers to sustainably manage their land and sell native products like guayusa than become involved in industrial agriculture, deforestation, or migrant labor. Double-blind control trials have shown that providing earned income to impoverished families is the most effective way to help them lift themselves out of poverty, and we were seeing that firsthand. (The book *Poor Economics: A Radical Rethinking of the Way to Fight Global Poverty* by Abhijit Banerjee and Esther Duflo is a great read on the topic.)

After hours of conversations and other social innovation exercises, we felt like we had it: "Improve Livelihoods for Amazonian Farming Families." We were not a charity giving handouts and thus disempowering the local people—we were being good businesspeople paying fair prices and giving them the opportunity to support their families in a way that they valued.

At the same time, we acknowledged that creating new markets alone does not automatically mean long-term positive impact for farmers. To best fulfill our vision, our hybrid organizational structure would give us more ability to address this question of "livelihoods" in a true way: beyond just income generation, we were working with farmers who were mostly new to markets and cash economies, and living in one of the most fragile and biodiverse ecosystems in the world.

While Runa's for-profit companies would drive new income to local communities by purchasing sustainable products, Runa

Foundation would work on more comprehensive strategies to support indigenous livelihoods. The nonprofit side would help develop and strengthen the farmer cooperatives to better negotiate and organize, research the most sustainable ways for farmers to grow guayusa, design sustainable land management plans for forest conservation, develop community savings and loan programs, and help start other sustainable value chains to benefit farming families.

We also decided that less than 5 percent of Runa Foundation's annual budget would come from Runa LLC, a somewhat radical move. Most companies would brag about how much they funded their foundations, but we wanted to do the opposite. We wanted the foundation to be autonomous and not beholden to the business, so that it could empower the farmers to push back against the company when necessary and uphold the highest standards always. We may be one of the few companies in the world to do this, but we felt this was the best way to minimize the danger of the foundation simply becoming a vehicle to make the company look good.

Moreover, the biggest impact that the company could create with its limited dollars was to build the biggest market possible for guayusa and the farmers. It made sense not to divert cash flow away from this focused objective and into Runa Foundation, assuming Runa Foundation was able to get its own funding.

Inspired by this vision, Eliot decided that, in addition to being schmucks, Dan and I had built a great platform for growth, shown deep integrity in our work, and exhibited the right degree of absurdity for his standards. When we formally offered him the position of not only executive director but also a cofounder of Runa Foundation, his response was "Yeah, I'm down."

Eliot moved to Quito and I vividly remember our first ride down to the jungle together. "So I'm not like y'all and that's *definitely* not gonna change," he cackled. (Eliot does a lot of cackling.) "Your whole 'work yourself into the ground and run a million miles an hour thing' isn't how I roll. I need space and breathing room to work. Just trust me."

While Francisco's workaholic nature was familiar and comfortable to me, giving Eliot the freedom to lead in his own style pushed all my boundaries. I recognized him as a visionary with a particular kind of focus. He clearly had the entrepreneurial capacity to build up Runa Foundation, and his charisma and passion as a leader was palpable, but his management style was TBD.

The first gargantuan task Eliot addressed along with Francisco and their teams was to get Runa full organic and Fair Trade certifications. This took a Herculean effort that included endless planning, training, and paperwork—sooooo much paperwork!

Whenever I hear people say *Oh, yeah, you know 'organic' doesn't really mean anything,* I start to hyperventilate and almost can't control myself. Organic certification is incredibly difficult to achieve, is very meaningful from a production and sustainability point of view, and would radically improve our intersecting planetary and health crises if taken more seriously, in my not-so-humble opinion. The same goes for Fair Trade.

With organic certification, the crux of the challenge for us was that the system was set up to certify farms and plantations growing products in a fixed plot, the norm for almost anything considered "agriculture." In contrast, we were working with over one thousand different farming families at the time, each with a tree here and a tree there throughout their forest gardens. We had to come up with an innovative model for defining the "agricultural plot" as a fifty-square-foot rectangle around each individual tree for the organic certification and then do that for one thousand farmers with proper GPS coordinates, maps, training programs, inspections, and, again, sooooo much paperwork!

With Fair Trade, we ran into different issues. Fairtrade International, the organization that grants Fair Trade certification, initially rejected us because the farmers were still in the process of organizing their legally registered cooperatives. At the time, Fair Trade would only work with either (1) fully registered, fully functioning farmers' cooperatives, or (2) big industrial plantations (in which case the Fair Trade benefits go to the plantation workers and employees).

This sits with the driving philosophy of Fair Trade, which has two fundamental tenets. The first is a guaranteed minimum price to farmers for their crops. The second, less-known, but very important requirement is what's called a "social premium" fund payment. It's an additional sum that a company pays on top of the Fair Trade minimum price. This is money that farmers and workers can then invest in social, environmental, and economic development projects to improve their communities as they see fit.

Given the newness of the guayusa supply chain, there was still some distance to go until the farmers could organize to the extent necessary to meet Fairtrade International's requirements, so there was no one to whom we could pay the social premium.

There are several organizations that confer Fair Trade certification. Fair Trade USA was once part of Fairtrade International but split off over disagreements in direction and became independent. Fair Trade USA wanted to innovate and expand the umbrella for the types of efforts that could get certification.

Working with them, we designed a system in which we would pay the standard 15 percent social premium on all the guayusa we purchased. This money would go into a fund administered by Fundación Runa, the Ecuadorian branch of the Runa Foundation, as a short-term solution, although its use would be determined democratically by committees elected by the farmers. The arrangement is slowly phasing out over time as the farmers establish their cooperatives to receive and administer the funds.

Maintaining the Space

Luis, Oscar, Nick, Francisco, Eliot—all of these early hiring and firing decisions were the hardest piece of the puzzle for me, because they were so *personal.* Letting go of people who had invested their lives in starting Runa with us felt awful, and trusting new team members with the future of our enterprise was terrifying. They were not carbon emission statistics, business plan projections, or some seedling experiment. These were my friends.

In the moment, the sharpness of these growing pains and doubts I felt about bringing people in and out of the organization were all very unsettling. As my go-to in stressful times, I spent more time by myself in the rainforest just sitting, walking, and thinking about these challenges.

As I pondered the parallels, it felt like creating a thriving *chakra* was strikingly similar to creating a healthy team. In a *chakra* the cultivation process begins with triggering the right conditions for growth (burning down an established forest). Next you *choose* what to let grow and what to weed out.

Organizational development can work essentially the same way. You have to create the conditions (business promise, team culture, compensation, etc.) to attract the right people to want to work with you, then clear the space for them to succeed. As the leader, you are the farmer. You have to identify the species you want, cut out the ones you don't, and constantly evaluate the balance as the forest garden takes shape.

In certain cases we definitely made bad hires and poor choices in bringing on the wrong people for specific roles and had to let them go. It's a difficult situation but also a natural process in a growing organization.

In addition to understanding the flows and cycles of growth, as the leader, like the farmer, you have to constantly negotiate the boundaries of your organization. "Negotiate" truly is the right word here. I negotiated everything from work style with Eliot, dress codes at the office with Francisco, how we would process guayusa leaves based on our available resources, compensation with every employee—the list goes on, but every step always required conversation, fluidity, and give-and-take on both sides. Your mission, your values, and your growth strategy should guide your machete. If a person or a plant is in alignment and fits within the ever-moving boundaries of the vision, they get more space and more sunlight. If not, they need to go.

This perspective might sound harsh, because it is. Leading isn't always fun, and having these conversations is usually horribly uncomfortable. That's why individuals who have the characteristics and training of a true leader are uniquely designed to take on the task, prioritizing the health, balance, and diversity of the entire system over any one element.

I wouldn't have put myself in the camp of being a leader with a capital *L* at that time. I feel like guayusa or something beyond was guiding me as best it could. We continually refined the boundaries of our organization and clarified our values, and little by little our whacky troop of pioneers seemed to be gaining ground.

Chapter 7

You Are the Offering

I'd been running on adrenaline for two years. As hard as it had been at times, our early work in Ecuador was also fun, full of novelty and adventure. Now it was time to head back to the States and not only start a new chapter for Runa but a personal one as well. The business was getting more and more "real" every day and would require ever more commitment and focus. While shamans will often advise you to open yourself and trust the process in ceremony, actually doing that can be excruciating. It can feel exactly the same way as your business begins to grow and demands more than you knew or thought you were ready to give.

In January 2011, I packed up the same backpack I'd arrived with in Ecuador and returned to the U.S. In the previous months there had been a few changes at Runa's U.S. "headquarters." Charlie, who had been working closely with Dan, had graduated from Brown and moved to San Francisco to work for Google, leaving Dan alone in Providence. Since most of our college friends had moved to New York, and Brooklyn was becoming an epicenter for artisanal foods, Dan decided to migrate down as well.

After arriving in Brooklyn, Dan had visited several potential office spaces and analyzed the pros and cons of each. Predictably, we just chose the cheapest one. It was on the fifth floor of an old seven-story bank building on Flatbush Avenue in downtown Brooklyn. Grandly titled "the Metropolitan Exchange" (MEx), it was advertised as a "cooperative of creative professionals" who "share clean, affordable office space that includes large common areas."

Creative and affordable? Yes. Clean? Not so much.

Our landlord was a lovable hoarder in his seventies named Al Attara whose cheerful manner and bushy white beard led Dan to nickname him "the Hipster Santa Claus." When you walked in, to even get to the elevator, you maneuvered around scattered paint cans, a fortune-telling weight scale, a pommel horse, some sixteen-foot-tall Greek columns that had been left by a theater group, and lots of mannequins. If anyone who we thought might come in a suit was coming over to meet with us, we emailed them a warning so they didn't go running for the hills when they entered.

We shared space with progressive urban planners, sustainable architects, some former Peace Corps volunteers importing Fair Trade chocolate from Madagascar (Madécasse, one of my favorite chocolates ever), and a woman making miniature cupcakes. At night a jazz collective used the space to rehearse while in the kitchen some food truck guys prepped for the next day. Paint was peeling off the walls, the air-conditioning didn't really work, and in the summer there was such an infestation of flies that we had to hang flypaper everywhere. The whole place pushed the concept of "cool" and "funky" Brooklyn into the zone of straight-up decrepit.

Each morning we arrived at work after passing the Army recruiting office and then the methadone clinic on Flatbush Avenue. We would fill some French presses with guayusa and start jamming on the tasks that were piling up on our ridiculously long and varied to-do lists.

Attracting Investors and Advisors

Chief among the tasks facing us was to find investors as fast as possible: for the majority of our first year in Brooklyn, we didn't have enough money at the start of each month to finish it. We needed to pay for consultants, product designers, office costs, website design, legal fees, flights back to Ecuador, and minimal salaries for ourselves just to get by. Fundraising was a matter of survival.

As we looked at how to accomplish this goal, we went back, yet again, to the spirit of the guayusa ceremony. We hoped that sticking to our values and focusing on the mission would help attract investors who shared the depth of our vision, although we feared they might think we had our heads in the wrong place and our mission would "dilute shareholder value."

One of our guest speakers in Danny Warshay's class at Brown was Bill Stone, a lawyer in Rhode Island who founded Outside

GC, an innovative firm that provides general-counsel legal services to companies on an as-needed basis. As a start-up, that means you can get help from high-level, experienced attorneys at a fraction of the cost of hiring a full-time general counsel or contracting with a huge law firm.

Bill possessed a wealth of knowledge when it came to start-up strategy, corporate structure, and fundraising, so we hit him up after graduation about what we were doing in Ecuador and continued to send him regular updates. As we progressed, Bill was impressed that we were actually making good on our plans and decided to help us with legal structure and fundraising strategy.

We'd learned that beverage companies are traditionally valued as a multiple of their gross revenue, with the average multiple being 3. So if a company is doing $30 million in annual revenue its valuation would be $90 million. We were what is euphemistically called in the start-up world "pre-revenue": in other words, we made no money. As such, we had no idea how to value our company for potential investors.

Bill taught us about "convertible debt," which I highly recommend to early-stage entrepreneurs. It lets you take loans from people with the promise to either pay the loan back in cash plus interest or later convert the loan into ownership shares of the company. That meant we didn't have to try to value the business early on, before we had revenues, and then risk selling shares at a price that was too low.

Just as importantly, it gave us flexibility to have "rolling closes." In normal equity financing where investors buy shares in a private company, you set out to raise a certain amount of money, get commitments from investors, and then set a closing date when the funds get transferred and the investment round "closes." With convertible debt we could meet an investor on a Monday, get a commitment from them on Tuesday, send them the documents on Wednesday, and get their money in our account by Friday (although it almost never happened that quickly).

We also "Runa-gized" the convertible debt structure to fit our goal of building a community of support around us. Conventional fundraising wisdom says that you want to take investments from as few people as possible so that your "cap table" (the list of shareholders in your company) doesn't become too long and unmanageable. It also says that you want to make sure all your investors are "strategic investors," meaning that they have relevant experience and can add concrete value to your business.

We threw both of these principles out the window, in part because we had to. Was there a long line of deep-pocketed strategic investors sprinting to 33 Flatbush Avenue and hurrying past the mannequins, pommel horse, and paint cans to write checks to build our obscure Amazonian tea company? No freaking way.

What we did have were friends and family members whom we could ask/convince/beg to invest relatively small amounts in our convertible debt round (as low as $5,000) and then ask them to introduce us to their friends and their friends' friends to do the same. With an operating budget of $20,000 to $30,000 a month, we were able to survive with this strategy. Fundamentally, we felt that the enthusiasm, connections, and advice we got from our community of investors was priceless.

One of the most personally meaningful checks we received

early on was from Pat, one of my best friends from Brown, who first introduced me to the concept of social entrepreneurship.

A reduced version of our conversation went something like this:

Pat: "You want my money? First, I don't have that much and, second, dude, you've never even had a job before . . ."

Me: "Yeah, I know, but we're gonna make this work."

Pat: "For some reason I *know* you will make it work. How? I have no fucking clue. I inherited some money from my grandparents and have saved a lot of what I earned working since high school, so I've got, like, $25,000 to my name. I think I'll give you, like, half of it."

From there, in true Runa spirit, we got in front of everyone we possibly could to either pitch, ask for advice, or usually some mix of the two. Our early success rate was abysmal, but we got better at pitching each time, becoming tighter, more precise, and more prepared for questions. The actual experience of going out and asking people for their money forced us to improve in a way that we never could have by just sitting in our office and practicing with each other.

We were advised early on that investors love entrepreneurs who know their numbers, so we got them down cold. That meant we could walk people through our projected P&L (profit and loss statement, the main financial statement showing revenue and spending projections) almost by heart, speak to exact production and guayusa conversion ratios from fresh leaf to dried leaf to tea bags and bottles without missing a beat, and rattle off beverage industry trends and category growth percentages in our sleep.

Impressing people with the details of our actual business

plan wasn't the goal. Everyone knew the plan would evolve and change, probably dramatically so, and that it would be impossible to see all the hurdles ahead. What this level of preparedness did show was, first, our determination and commitment, and second, our ability to think.

Good things soon followed. One of our early interns' best friend's father was a successful executive named Tim Sullivan, who was about to retire after three decades of working for Pepsi, where he ran factories and logistics around the world. He heard about Runa from our intern's friend and reached out to us to learn more. Dan had a preliminary Skype call with Tim, who, in his very sharp, methodical, and composed way asked all types of pointed questions about our prospects. When it was over, Dan told me, "That guy's supersmart. There's no way he'll invest in us."

We were elated when he followed up and said he loved hearing about the business and wanted to be part of it. He ended up investing a substantial amount in Runa and even flew down to Ecuador with me to help figure out how to scale production. The timing was perfect: Tim was truly passionate about logistical problem solving and supply chain development, and as he headed into retirement, we offered a way for him to continue doing what he loved in service of a mission he believed in.

We invited Tim to formally join our fledgling board of advisors, which would prove to be a critical pillar of our early success in the U.S. We had already roped in our former professors Danny Warshay and Alan Harlam; Bill Stone from Outside GC; and Bob Burke, the former VP of sales from Stonyfield Farm who had advised us on our original business plan.

From our point of view, the advisory board was like the council of elders in our guayusa ceremony, imparting wisdom, gifting advice, and teaching us the ins and outs of our new world. While the guidance itself was essential, the mere *existence* of the advisory board also helped with fundraising. The "Sure, we don't know jack BUT we're smart (enough), we'll work until we're sick, AND we have this super-experienced board of advisors who we listen to religiously" line was a good one.

One way Dan and I helped attract and keep good advisors was by doing our very best to follow through on their advice, even if we didn't end up agreeing with them. For example, if Tim suggested that we look into five things, we looked into them, did them all, and then told him the outcome of our efforts, what we learned, and the challenges we'd had.

Alternatively, if Danny advised that we look to create a stock option pool in a certain way, but we decided to do it another way, we would get back to Danny and tell him what we learned from his advice and why our analysis (or conflicting advice from another advisor) made us opt to go in a different direction. Following through like this sends a message to people who are very busy that their time is valued in the most concrete way possible: by acting on it.

The quarterly newsletters we sent to advisors and investors were another key tool. These, we learned, should be as clear, concise, and actionable as possible, and always sent in the body of an email, not as an attachment. We designed a bullet-point template to relay the most important news in each area of the business: sales, marketing, operations, and finance. Most importantly, we always ended each update with sections titled "What's Not Working" and then "How You Can Help."

While the job of our newsletters was of course to rally enthusiasm and excitement from our investors and advisors, we also decided to be honest about where we were struggling. To be vulnerable is to be real, to build trust and create confidence in what matters most. Everyone fully expects that there will be problems with a start-up, and I've heard investors say that they're often turned off by entrepreneurs who can't exit the "Everything is AMAZING! We are KILLING IT!" loop. Besides that, we learned that one of the most rewarding parts of the process for our investors was being able to use their expertise to help us when some issue was punching us in the face.

After a while, it became hard to think of new and creative ways to say "We really need money" in the "How You Can Help" section of our updates. In practice, what we found to be most successful is that after we would talk to a friend, a mentor, an advisor, or even a random person at a trade show who liked us, we would always ask, "Who else do you know who would be willing to speak with us and that we could learn from? Would you be able to introduce us to a few people? We would very much appreciate it."

Our first investor who wasn't a family member or a friend came through a woman Jose Stevens had introduced me to. She connected me to a mortgage broker in the Bay Area she thought would be into what we were doing. "His name is Richard," she said. "I'm sure I can get him to at least meet with you."

As it happened, we had helped bring Alejandro up to the Bay Area at that time for some promotional events to spread the word about guayusa. Thinking that Richard would be excited to meet Alejandro and that it would only help our fundraising pitch, I dragged him along when I went to meet with Richard at his office in Marin County.

Richard was a middle-aged man, with receding white hair and sharp eyes. I was a twenty-three-year-old kid, and Alejandro came to the meeting wearing a headband and carrying his flute.

We served Richard some overbrewed tea from a thermos and gave a scattered talk about the meaning of guayusa to Ecuadorian indigenous communities and the enormous opportunity for this random leaf as a consumer beverage. Alejandro decided to play his flute for Richard, and I caught some baffled looks from other brokers and secretaries walking by the conference room.

What we didn't know was that Richard is a deeply spiritual person, having studied in India for years. As he described it, he laughed to himself when we walked out, but then did a "deeper check-in," which was basically meditating on the opportunity and looking for intuitive advice from the powers beyond rationality. The unexpected response? An overwhelming yes.

Richard's conscious reaction was *Really? You sure? Give money to the kid and the headband guy with the flute?* However, he trusted that on a deeper level there was something to what we were doing. He called us the next day to say he was going to invest $25,000.

Other investors simply show that you never know who has the money.

At a street fair in Williamsburg, Brooklyn, Dan and I had a table where, in our guayusa-powered, high-energy way, we offered samples of "a rare Amazonian tea" to everyone who passed. A twenty-two-year-old guy named Eden, who was volunteering to help with crowd control, came up to us and said, "Wow! You guys really hustle! Tell me about your business."

Originally from Taiwan, he was in New York working for an investment bank. He ended up investing in Runa after he spent a few months getting to know us.

When I visited Quito, I always tried to take our ever-growing posse of interns out for ceviche. On one trip, there was a twenty-year-old guy from the Czech Republic named Ladi. When I asked him how he ended up interning for us, he said he'd seen a video on the Internet about Runa and thought it would be cool to work with us. "The last few years have been pretty intense," he said, "and I wanted to take a break and do something different."

He explained that he had taken over his mom's struggling commodities trading company at age seventeen, after her father became ill and she began taking care of him around the clock. Working sixteen to twenty hours a day, he turned it into a $30 million annual business. The stress had been getting to him, so he took some time off to hang out in South America. As I was wondering why this guy was interning for me instead of the other way around, he asked, "Hey, do you have any investment opportunities?"

One of the most effective tools I found for gaining early traction with potential investors was to have a well-designed and to-the-point investor presentation that included a detailed explanation of guayusa's benefits, beverage industry trends, the structure of our business, and future growth projections. I was surprised to learn that some investors didn't even read the business plan and simply used the overview deck as their main portal for understanding the business. I highly recommend that all organizations spend a meaningful amount of time creating a compelling pitch deck: I'm certain it was one of the key elements that were critical to our early fundraising.

Surrender

In college, I vowed I would never live in New York City. I viewed myself as a more outdoorsy "West Coast" type of guy, and the big city was definitely not for me. No way, not ever.

I loved Ecuador. There was an innate vibrancy and warmth in the culture, especially among the Kichwa communities I'd spent so much time in. New York City, by contrast, seemed to be all about money, success, and striving—not necessarily bad things, but astringent when distilled into such a concentrated form. Every day, as I rode the subway to work in the early morning, this severity hit me again like a Taser stuck right in my gut.

I was in a position I'd never imagined: not only living in New York City but working Wall Street–type hours around the clock. The only difference between us and the recent college grads working as bankers was that they were getting fat paychecks and bonuses, while we were frantically fundraising to avoid going bankrupt.

I began to yearn for the direct and tangible connection I felt to our mission that I had in Ecuador. Being far away from the Amazon, there was a danger that our mission would slip from feeling visceral to something more theoretical.

To keep that connection vibrant, I tried a few things. First, I convinced friends to get up very early to join me for guayusa sessions. We would rally on Vanderbilt Avenue in Fort Greene at our friend Matt Palevsky's apartment before sunrise to share our dreams, tell jokes, and chug guayusa before going to work.

I also arranged 5:00 a.m. Skype chats ("Guayu-Skypes" as

we came to call them) between our staff and interns in Brooklyn and our team in Ecuador, so that we could reflect on and laugh about each other's latest challenges and successes and the peculiarities of our shared work that bound us—worlds together and worlds apart. Eventually, we also set up similar Skype chats with farmers in retail stores (though not at 5:00 a.m.) to build bridges between customers and the farmers.

Still, the work in New York—not only fundraising but figuring out packaging, distribution, marketing, FDA approvals, etc.—was a grind that required nearly all my waking attention, and I worried I was becoming less "spiritual" in the process.

I called Jose Stevens and confided how I was feeling, that the work was overtaking me and I wasn't offering enough in my spiritual life. "Tyler," he said, "right now, *you* are the offering. The work you're doing is the offering. The blood, sweat, and tears you're putting into this company are your prayer. There is no more real prayer than what you are doing."

It was a very helpful way of reframing it. For nonreligious people, we often think of prayer as something impractical, otherworldly, or hopeful at best. In contrast, from the shamanic perspective, prayer is understood and specifically valued as something practical. With any prayer, the ultimate goal is to call forth into physical reality a vision or intention. Prayer is far from passive. Once you have prayed for something, it is time to step up and take concrete steps toward that goal. The more devotion and commitment you put in, the more likely you are to make it happen. It seems that the deeper forces of life, in my experience, conspire in unseen, often strange ways to support the concentrated bursts of intention and dedication we offer up through our heartfelt work.

If at First You Don't Succeed . . .

With our constant money problems, we wanted to get some type of product to market as quickly as we could. Although our long-term plan centered on making ready-to-drink products in bottles or cans, the least risky and least capital-intensive way to start was with guayusa tea bags.

After starting to work through the myriad of packaging, design, and positioning questions on our own, we connected with a highly regarded design agency that had a passion for working with social enterprises. However, we quickly learned—and have learned ever more so over time—that agencies are only as good as you set them up to be. We were all over the place with the direction we gave them, but generally focused on the guayusa ceremony, traditional Kichwa art, and esoteric indigenous philosophy. So, not surprisingly, we ended up with a distinctly tribal design for our first products, inspired by paintings on Kichwa pottery.

Designs in hand, we lined up our first production run at a "co-packer" (a manufacturing plant that makes products for other companies on an as-needed basis), having purchased boxes, tea bags, tea bag tags, tea bag envelopes, tea bag string, and cardboard cases for assembly at their facility.

Our advisor Bob Burke introduced us to a guy named Steve Verde, the former VP of eastern region sales for United Natural Foods, the largest natural foods distributor in the country, where he had managed over a billion dollars in revenue. Steve was a total wise guy and loved to mess with us and pull pranks, so we got along wonderfully. Whenever I would do something stupid, his favorite reply was: "What more can you expect from a jock from Brown?"

We hired him as our outsourced sales manager to set up meetings for us with key retailers and help us plan our go-to-market strategy. Another advantage of having him on retainer as a consultant was that we could—with a little bit of a stretch—refer to him as our "vice president of sales," which further helped with fundraising.

Steve had a great relationship with Rachel, the head buyer for the New York region of Whole Foods, and managed to get us a meeting at their annual "category review" for hot tea and coffee. Many retail chains have a very strict calendar for when they review different product categories each year, so if we missed this opportunity, we would have to wait another twelve months before we could get in front of her.

The approximately four hundred Whole Foods stores in the U.S. are divided into eleven different regions, and the individual buyer for each has tremendous autonomy (although that is now starting to change): you could view them as demi-gods with the power to make or break your brand. We were told that Rachel, the buyer for the New York region, was notorious for not suffering fools, so it was vital that we make our presentation bulletproof.

We'd decided that it would be really nice to use premium pyramid tea bags but didn't have enough time to get proper envelopes (the wrapper around each individual tea bag) made for them. Instead, the only thing we could find at the last minute were some extra-large, very cheap-looking plastic envelopes similar to what you'd find around a fortune cookie. Because of their size, we had to use a huge box.

We managed to convince a friend's print shop in Providence to rush-print a sample box for us, which Steve picked up the day before the meeting and stuffed with tea bag samples.

The night before our meeting, I stayed over at my girlfriend's parents' apartment in Manhattan, leaving at 5:30 in the morning to make my way uptown on the subway, then over the George Washington Bridge on a bus to meet Steve at a diner in Fort Lee, New Jersey. Still being new to the city, I got lost on the subway, missed my bus connection, and had to sprint from the bus terminal to the diner, where I jumped into Steve's car and we sped to the meeting. Thanks to Steve's intrepid driving, we arrived only a minute late for our 9:00 a.m. appointment.

As we walked into the office, I repeated our pitch in my head, feeling like a feudal peasant preparing to petition a lord. I sat down, took a deep breath, and started with "This product comes straight from the heart of the Amazon . . ." Hoping for some show of excitement at what I thought was a wildly ingenious hook, my stomach tightened as Rachel's face registered no response.

I planned the whole pitch so that there was a grand reveal at the end, but only after I had explained the importance of guayusa to the Kichwa people. Unfortunately, we weren't given as long as our team had gotten during our final pitch in Danny Warshay's class at Brown. Rachel cut off my hype after about fifteen seconds.

"So, anyway, what's the product?" she asked.

Steve opened his bag and handed me the box to pass over to her. As it hit my hand, I felt something on it and looked down to see that a rubber band was the only thing holding the box together. I froze. After giving Steve a look of *You've got to be fucking kidding me!* I slid the package across the table.

She reached down, saw the rubber band, and ripped it off. The box collapsed like a house of cards, tea bags wrapped in cheap cellophane falling on her lap.

She looked at me, and then at Steve, and then back at me.

"I think we're done here," she said.

Ouch. One of those big sucker-punches-to-the-gut-that-knocks-the-wind-out-of-you kind of ouches. As I traced back through the decisions we'd made to end up with such a blunder, desperately looking for lessons I could take away, I found about fifteen things we could have done differently, any one of which would have avoided the error. But the ultimate root cause was that we were running and gunning, and when you're running and gunning, your aim just isn't going to be spot-on.

The number of balls we had in the air was ludicrous, but "just slowing down" and being more patient didn't feel like an option either. So what were we to do? I figured that I couldn't necessarily control whether or not the metaphorical wheels of Runa would ever gain traction and propel us forward, but I could ensure that the wheels were spinning as fast as humanly possible. And whenever our wheels did get traction, I could make damn sure we would get the biggest jolt possible.

That was the theory, at least, and over time I've learned more graceful evolutions of this approach. But as twenty-five-year-olds trying to make it in the big city, putting our heads back down and continuing to hustle was indeed what got us that ultimate traction.

A few months later, we convinced a friend of a friend to give us a two-foot-by-three-foot space on a table at the end of their booth for the annual Summer Fancy Food Show at the Javits Center in New York. A giant showcase for some 180,000 specialty food products—essentially any type of cheese, spice, pasta, oil, tea, or coffee you can think of—the Fancy Foods Show is like Disneyland for specialty food.

Dan and I stood in the aisle, excitedly asking everyone who passed by, "Hey there! Would you like to try some Amazonian tea?"

A serious-seeming woman with a clipboard stopped and looked us over. Her name badge was flipped over so we had no idea who she was. "Why not?" she said.

We poured her a cup and she took a sip, rolling it around in her mouth as we told her a bit about the company.

She took another taste and thought for a moment. "This is incredible," she said. "You guys missed our last Category Review, but we can cut this in off-cycle. Send me samples and pricing ASAP."

She gave us her card. We were shocked to see that she was the buyer for Whole Foods' mid-Atlantic region.

Chapter 8

Know Your Shadow

As elated as we were about getting into Whole Foods, it also dialed up the pressure. It was vital that we make the best of our opportunity in the chain's mid-Atlantic region, since all the other regions of Whole Foods would look at our sales there to determine if we were worth their while. If we didn't do well, there wasn't much hope we'd make it into any of the other areas—or any other retailers for that matter.

I thought that getting our first taste of success as a business would have been relieving and rewarding, but it only seemed to highlight the lack of growth we'd yet to achieve. We felt even *more* pressured to capitalize on the newfound momentum. Given our dogged determination to get those results, we did indeed make progress.

Kicking into gear, we hired our first U.S. employees: Caroline Turnbull, who, at twenty-three, was just out of college; and Anna Premo, the eldest of our crew at twenty-seven. Caroline's focus was supposed to be sales and Anna's marketing, but the four of us all ended up tackling everything together.

The Whole Foods mid-Atlantic region includes Pennsylvania, New Jersey, Delaware, Maryland, Washington, D.C., Virginia, West Virginia, Ohio, and Kentucky. With boxes of Runa on the shelves in stores, the most valuable tool we had was the ability to go into stores, talk with managers, and serve samples to customers.

Dan, Caroline, Anna, and I spent a few months traveling the region, setting up demo tables at stores and "hawking the guayguay," as we liked to say. Caroline generously volunteered to go all the way out to Kentucky and sleep at campgrounds in her tent to help us save money.

With a few pump pot dispensers full of our different flavors, we would pour small sample cups for people and hand out informational postcards. It wasn't always fun to stand for hours on end and cheerily annoy passing shoppers to try our tea, but the payoff was invaluable on two levels.

First, we were doing the most clearly measurable and results-oriented marketing possible. Advertising with billboards or even social media can be difficult, because you don't know how these "shotgun" marketing efforts actually drive sales at retail. Additionally, if you only have three Whole Foods that sell Runa in Washington, D.C., compared to maybe ten thousand stores that sell Pepsi, what good does generalized marketing do when no one can find our product?

In stark contrast, if we served someone a sample and they said, "I like it, where can I get one?" we would hand them a box from the store's inventory, and they would place it in their cart and go directly to checkout. If the store had thirty boxes on the shelf when we showed up to sample, and five were left afterward, we knew exactly the return on investment of our marketing and that we were driving concrete sales.

The second benefit was direct consumer feedback. Rather than hypothesizing about what our target demographic would think about the product or looking at sales reports on a computer, we were chatting with hundreds and hundreds of consumers every week, hearing what they liked about the product and why, learning about their tea and energy drink consumption habits, discovering how their purchasing decisions were affected by pricing and special promotions . . . the list goes on.

We quickly learned that you can tell if people don't like the sample, because they always say the same sort of thing every time: "Interesting . . ." or "Hmmm. That's, uh, *unique.* Thank you." And then they walk away.

Thankfully, most people loved the flavor of guayusa as well as the fact that it was sustainably grown in the Amazon. We found, however, that the story was somewhat vague for most people. They had no personal ties to South America, or didn't really know exactly where Ecuador was, and some were confused about the whole concept of "indigenous farmers." I was literally asked once, "Ecuador, right. So where exactly in Africa is that again?" As nice as it might have sounded, the story was not enough to drive people to load up on boxes of Runa.

After spending a few years intensely focused on building a company that would benefit indigenous farmers, we naturally assumed other people would feel the same passion. It was a little disappointing when they didn't.

The selling point that hit home the most was when we told people that guayusa would give them "a sustained lift of energy," better than a cup of coffee. For people who didn't like coffee or were looking to cut down on their intake, these magic words were enough to spur them to throw a box in their cart. Life is crazy and it's not getting less crazy for anyone. People need energy to get them through the day, can't afford crashing or getting tweaked out, and are increasingly open and hungry for new options.

It was a real-time demonstration of a concept we'd learned from Barbara Tannenbaum, a public speaking professor at Brown, who said that the most important thing when giving a presentation is to figure out the one question the audience will definitely want answered: *What's in it for me?* ("WIIFM" for short.) It turned out that when our proposed WIIFM was helping farmers and the environment, it wasn't immediate, tangible, or relatable to most consumers, but great-tasting tea that will carry you through the day better than coffee was.

Additionally, we had started doing more laboratory analysis of guayusa leaves, and the data was extremely encouraging. In addition to having high levels of naturally occurring caffeine, guayusa contains polyphenols, flavonoids, and particularly high amounts of chlorogenic acids, which studies have shown to improve cardiovascular health, reduce high blood pressure, and prevent fat accumulation. With both the legitimacy of the chemistry data and our WIIFM epiphany, we changed our messaging to focus our sampling pitch around health and energy, and our sales began to climb.

We also applied the skill set we acquired earlier in our journey in Ecuador and "shape-shifted" to each shopper's needs, pitching

Runa as a "pre-workout" drink when talking to consumers who had supplements in their carts and clearly looked like they hit the gym, talking about the "notes of molasses, caramel, chicory with a hint of natural sweetness" when talking to chic, stylish consumers with expensive cheese and wine in their carts, and telling the Kichwa farmer story when talking to yoga moms with Fair Trade chocolate and premium coconut water in their carts. Although we weren't around a fire at sunrise, as we handed out our samples, it did somehow feel like we were invoking the indigenous tradition of weaving stories over cups of guayusa.

We discovered so much from giving out samples in stores that I always encourage new entrepreneurs to try to get a product to market as quickly as possible, get feedback from real people, and hone it from there. I understand the temptation to wait until you feel everything is perfect, but the danger is that you might hold off only to eventually find that your conception of the product doesn't click with actual customers. You can't learn as much on paper or in your head as you can when you're staring at your product on an actual shelf with a price tag underneath it. Better to learn that sooner rather than later, welcome the challenges, and navigate up the hill.

#FacebookFail

That said, one important caveat is that you should only roll out your product (or service) on a small, accessible scale so that you can truly learn and then make refinements. Before you get too big, you first want to be able to understand how changes really affect sales and, second, make those changes.

That goes with the prevailing wisdom in the food and beverage industry, which is to start with one market or retailer and then concentrate on getting your story, packaging, and placement right. Then, when you scale, you want to go "a mile deep and an inch wide," meaning that you stay focused on either one city, one region, or even one "channel of trade," as it's called—only natural food stores, only conventional supermarkets, etc.

While we conceptually understood that logic, Dan and I didn't feel we had the time to follow it. Just keeping ourselves afloat each month continually drained our bank account. In Ecuador too we had families growing guayusa with the expectation that we were going to buy it. It made for an intense pressure to produce revenues. It was hard to see, let alone critique, our desire to push forward rapidly, because the story wasn't about our own need to make money but *We need to make good on our commitments to these farmers.*

In the world of consumer packaged goods, there are really only two basic levers you can pull to grow a business. One is by increasing same store sales (known as "turns" or "velocity"); the other is by expanding distribution into new accounts (adding new "doors"). Increasing turns requires you to build the brand reputation and is done through methods such as offering in-store samples. It's by far the best way to go, but it takes time. Boosting doors simply means getting more distribution deals, which is what we unwisely jumped into.

There are huge risks to overexpansion. One, which we experienced, is that in desperation you can agree to deals that eat your margins or require you to be, let's say, "overly generous," to get into new accounts. One of the formal industry terms for "overly generous" is "slotting fees," which means to get your product into a store, you have to either write them a check to "slot" your products on the shelf or give them their entire first order for free (sometimes the second one too), at your loss.

Just as bad, the product is out there before the packaging and brand concept have been refined. So you end up overextended with a product that is not presented as well as it could be, and then have to overinvest to support stores that aren't ready for your products in the first place.

Our constant worrying about how to get meaningful revenue so that we could raise a real round of investment and avoid becoming failures before our friends and families led to some poor decisions.

In the middle of our drive to expand, we arranged to have a booth at the World Tea Expo in, of all places, Las Vegas, a huge yearly gathering of hundreds of tea companies, distributors, and industry experts. We hoped that it would be a great opportunity to showcase Runa and make connections.

Right before going to the show, I drank and enjoyed some tea samples a small company had sent us. I knew they were going to be at the Expo and wanted to meet them, so I went on their Facebook wall and wrote how much I liked that particular blend.

At that point I had an idea: Why not write on the Facebook walls of *all* the companies that will be at the expo? Wouldn't that help get Runa's name out there? Wasn't that a scrappy, hustling way to do business?

So, with the help of an intern, we looked on the websites of hundreds of companies to find a unique blend they offered, then posted on each company's Facebook wall about how much I liked one of their unique blends, adding a comment at the end with our booth number at the expo and an invitation to come by. Then, in the hectic days leading up to the trip, I pretty much forgot about it.

The expo was at the Las Vegas Convention Center, in a gargantuan hall lined with row upon row of booths manned by companies selling everything from packaging materials to manufacturing equipment to broker services and, of course, every kind of tea you can possibly imagine.

We were really proud of the booth we built, which was designed like an Amazonian hut, with a bamboo frame and a fresh leaf roof made from palm fronds we'd grabbed outside the convention center. To add to the experience, we had a blowgun from Ecuador that people could use to shoot darts at a board with a Runa logo on it. With our new glass teapots full of freshly brewed guayusa kept warm by candles underneath, we looked sharp in our new Runa shirts and excitedly waited for the first customers to arrive.

Not long after opening, a guy came to our booth and asked, "Who's Tyler?"

After I introduced myself, he said that he'd seen my post on his company's Facebook wall. For a moment I thought my plan had worked: here we were already making connections! What a great way to get our name out there!

But when he started asking me specific questions about which blend of his tea I had tried and why I had liked it, I started to feel sick. As I mumbled a few answers, a look of contempt came over his face.

"I was suspicious about your post on our wall, so I looked at your posting history and saw that you wrote on dozens of walls," he said. "You're full of shit." The worst part was, I couldn't even argue the point.

Orienting to the Underworld

As stupid as I felt at that moment, I was eventually grateful that he'd called me out. As we were struggling to get Runa off the ground, it was really easy to focus on our mission and all the good we intended to do. Left unchecked, this led to a temptation toward an "Ends justify the means"–type of thinking. After all, what was cutting a few corners if it meant that hundreds of indigenous farmers would lead better lives? Wasn't saving the Amazon worth a few harmless white lies here and there?

Alas, here comes the shadow, a dear teacher I was all too eager to do without. (Warning: Get ready to go down a shamanic wormhole here.)

Without a doubt, my favorite word in the Shipibo language is *caya*. It has three meanings: "shadow," "reflection," and "soul," with profound bridges of wisdom connecting the three definitions. The etymology of the word is *ca*, the Shipibo word for "go," and *ya*, meaning "with." Your soul is that which goes with you everywhere. Makes sense. Your shadow *also* goes with you wherever you go. To have a soul is to have a shadow, meaning the "shadow self" (not your physical shadow).

The portal to the soul, from this perspective, is the shadow itself, a doorway that is at once familiar and strange. One of my later Shipibo teachers always says, "The very first thing that happens when you use sacred medicines that connect to your soul is that your shadow comes forward."

The psychologist Carl Jung called our shadows the "subconscious containers" where we hide all the drives, feelings, and emotions that embarrass us or that we view as negative.

Modern psychology would discuss repressed fears, forgotten and denied contents of the psyche, and even collective angst about the difficulty of being human as part of the subconscious psychological forces that influence us in every moment. But in the world of shamanism, theory is quite useless, so the language and approach to these same forces is made more vivid and interactive, creating the potential to actively *relate* to, incorporate, and heal the shadow.

Basic human nature is to relegate uncomfortable aspects of ourselves to the shadow in order to pretend they don't exist: seek pleasure, avoid pain. However, the glitch in the operating system is that these aspects of ourselves seep in through our dreams, compulsive behaviors, paranoias, anxieties, and limiting beliefs about ourselves. Jung wrote that the less we understand our shadow, the darker it is and the more likely it is to drive our actions. The shamanic approach dovetails with Jung's, holding that just as there is day and night, and winter and summer, light and dark are inevitably part of our beings. In short, you can't be a complete human being without acknowledging and incorporating both. And if the shadow actually follows you everywhere you freaking go no matter what, then best to make friends with it.

From the Shipibo point of view, simply accessing the shadow is very easy. Go sit in the jungle all night by yourself. Done. Do literally anything that makes you afraid or uncomfortable. Mission accomplished. So the very sensitive, subtle, tricky, and challenging game is learning how to be present with the shadow without collapsing into, fighting with, running away from, or getting hijacked by it.

A little darkness can be useful, but too much at one time is totally overwhelming and even dangerous. This was apparent in the way I'd seen the Shipibo shamans working with various plant medicines, where they explicitly invoked a connection with the light and healing properties of a plant before working with it. Even though they would use these plants for healing, the Shipibo didn't see them as being purely filled with light, benevolence, wholesome intentions, and endless rainbows. To the contrary, they recognized the power these plants have to invoke both darkness and light. Rather than being "good" on their own, the Shipibo regard these plants as agnostic, even amoral, in their static state. Through specific prayers, songs, and "conversations" with the plant spirits, they say that each can be properly directed and oriented. The idea isn't necessarily that the dark side is "bad" and that you should avoid it but that you need to be *prepared* to work with it.

Tobacco, for example, is a "shadow master" sacred plant with both powerful light and dark sides. For indigenous people, it's a plant with a profound ability to strengthen, straighten, clarify, open, and manifest, and has been the most widely used sacred plant in the history of human civilization. When used in prayer, it is believed to amplify the intentions behind the prayer and communicate them on subtle levels to the power of the great mystery beyond.

Regardless of its stature as a "sacred" plant, tobacco is also seen to be "of the shadows." Quite literally the plant is known as a nightshade (a member of the Solanaceae family), and from a shamanic perspective its orientation is said to be toward the subconscious. It is seen to be highly programmable, both a sponge and an amplifier.

People in the modern world use tobacco to tamp down anxiety and escape from stress. The plant itself is degraded, as it is grown with pesticides and then processed into cigarette tobacco with chemicals such as formaldehyde and arsenic. Without any reverence or positive intentionality invoked in its production or usage, the intention and invocation become the underlying fear and anxiety the smoker brings to the experience, making the tobacco a vehicle for addiction and illness.

While shamans have long seen the dual nature of tobacco, it's interesting that modern scientific studies have found a "dual reinforcement model" in nicotine addiction. In other words, nicotine is not only itself addictive, it also sets off a number of chemical responses that further reinforce the addiction. For example, studies have found that if you smoke to relieve stress, the nicotine actually triggers secondary neurological responses in your brain that really do reduce stress, making you that much more addicted to using nicotine to get the stress relief.

A menacing, shamanically poetic interpretation would say that the tobacco has turned on you and is taking your lack of will to face the underlying anxiety as an offering to it. With that offering in hand, the tobacco uses your anxiety against you, further weakening your ability to find constructive ways to relate to your anxiety in the first place. While this is clearly hypothetical, it does beg the inverse question of whether using tobacco with positive intentions then reinforces those good feelings, which is what the shamans would claim.

You can use an axe to split wood for a fire, or you can use an axe to inflict harm. Intention is the deciding factor. Intention—the more refined and empowered the better—is the "nurture" that intersects with the "nature" of any medicine. With intention, you can be clear about your purpose for entering or exploring a shadow element before you go there. In this way you can access feelings of anger, mistrust, grief, and other shadow emotions without giving yourself over to them.

For Shipibo shamans, "dark" plants or "dark" energies are ones that *must* be programmed because of their receptive natures. Tobacco is addictive—it's a dangerous game on its own. A simple parallel highlights the basic idea: Would you ever hire an employee or executive you knew was very powerful and just let them loose with no job description, no training, no goals, and no reporting structure?

The Shipibo view of marijuana was of special interest to me, since I had relied on it so much to escape depression and anxiety during my first year of college. One of my later Shipibo teachers would always begin his explanations about a plant, person, or opportunity with: "*Cuando lo examinas bien* . . ." ("When you examine it closely . . ."). From a shamanic perspective, superficial appearances or effects are never to be trusted, and you must look at the core intentions and origins of anything you consume or relate to: the platitude "The road to hell is paved with good intentions" applies here.

Another one of my favorite sayings, learned from a Native American elder, is: "White man medicine makes you feel good, then makes you feel bad. Red man medicine makes you feel bad, then makes you feel good." The Shipibo would say this is actually the line between a "drug" and a "medicine" as well. Drugs help you skip over the real problem and provide temporary relief by offering an illusion of goodness. Yet, simultaneously, they create space for the illness, pain, or confusion to root itself in further. Medicines take you right into the pain and, if successful, uproot it from the source.

So while the effects of marijuana can be calming, relieving, sensual, and heartfelt, the plant is, literally, sticky, and that can be mirrored in its effects: it generally envelops you in a hazy fuzz. To shamans, whose entire healing philosophy centers around cleaning, opening, and aligning, a plant that is hazy and sticky goes completely against that intention. The actual psycho-spiritual mechanism of marijuana, they say, is to "cross your mind" and actually plug up your channels, disconnect you, and thereby produce a type of euphoria or transient clarity—the basic mechanism of a "drug."

While marijuana can unlock some doors of perception and produce insights, opening the doors of perception is not the goal from their point of view. In contrast, for modern people who live in largely repressed societies with little to no opportunities for consciousness expansion, the simple act of deepening connection to sensuality, the heart, laughter, and a sacred feeling of life can be an incredible blessing. Smoking weed in high school gifted me some of my first experiences of feeling the spirit of life, the magic of the universe, and the power of love.

But when the Shipibo shamans have dozens and dozens of plants to accomplish this same goal in what they would say is a more spiritually sound fashion, the appeal just isn't there. The dangers of getting caught in the plant's fuzzy grip outweigh any benefits it might have. A critical note is that no part of their perspective has any moral judgment. They're generally quite libertarian in my experience and avoid saying what someone should or shouldn't do. Their advice is to just understand the deeper layers of association and look more broadly at the effects of anything you do.

The Shadow of Shamanism

I'd like to make a quick and unfortunately necessary note here about the shadow of shamanic practice in the Amazon, and likely more broadly. One of the best pieces of advice I received when I first went to Peru was from my friend David, who said, "It's more accurate to think of these shamans as surgeons and not as gurus."

It took me a long time to see for myself what he meant, but he couldn't have been more on target. He meant that even though shamans work with subtle layers of energies and work in "spiritual" ways, our Western assumptions of what it means to be "spiritual" should not be projected. The shamans have rigorously trained in a highly sophisticated system of spiritual healing that, as Jose Stevens puts it, is primarily about power and not about enlightenment.

Intensive shamanic training requires incredible precision and calculation, and sometimes generates an almost inhuman detachment strikingly parallel to the mind-sets of modern-day surgeons. These practices can lead to incredible levels of wisdom, integrity, compassion, and generosity, but that's not always the case. The main goal is efficacy of treatment: eliminating disease.

Shamans are humans that have their own issues and limitations like everyone else, but also should be recognized as having a very different orientation to life than your average person. (Lord knows that if I was isolated in the jungle drinking intense plant medicines since I was eight years old, I'd be an even weirder dude than I already am.)

A false assumption of integrity and spiritual wisdom has led far too many foreigners into being manipulated, deceived, mistreated, abused, and exploited, both physically and spiritually, at the whims of shamans who lack basic integrity. The dark shadow of sexual abuse and manipulation by male shamans in the Amazon is far too real, and it truly breaks my heart. I've had several close friends fall victim to these abuses of power and at times it has made me want to renounce these traditions altogether.

In my personal opinion, power should never trump integrity, and anyone looking to work with a shaman or anyone with seemingly "mystical powers" should do so cautiously. Moreover, lots of "shamans" are indeed quacks, with little of the extensive training needed to work effectively.

So do your due diligence, trust your gut, and get recommendations from people you trust. Maintain healthy boundaries and never be deceived into thinking you need to compromise your own will and sense of what is right.

I wish I didn't see the need to share these sobering reflections, but ignoring the shadow only makes it stronger.

The Shadow of Entrepreneurship

Translating this whacky riff back to the business world, entrepreneurship is an activity whereby the very idea of the shadow is complete heresy. When you're starting a new business, it's summer all the time and the emphasis is on growth, heat, intensity, and light. When you've made that vulnerable leap into a new venture, it's almost a necessity to stress everything positive and downplay everything that's challenging, to keep yourself sane and to "fake it till you make it."

This isn't a terrible strategy. In many ways, success relies on this willful banishment of doubts and dark thoughts. The problem is that, with too much sun, you inevitably end up getting burned.

I was definitely in this rut. Working my personal shit out in ceremony had become familiar to me at this point, but I felt like I needed to find ways to access a similar space of self-discovery and healing within the realm of my everyday business duties.

So I started to work with Ryan Eliason, an executive coach based in Santa Cruz. He had a strong spiritual bent and a soft, reassuring manner that was welcoming, sincere, and connecting. Our Skype meetings had the feeling of a ceremony to me, creating a space to explore the deeper anxieties I was feeling—though he often had to work to get me there.

One morning he started our session by asking, "What do you feel in your body?"

It made me a little uncomfortable. I answered that I was "concerned" about how, if X didn't happen soon, then Y might not ever happen, and if Y never happened, then yada yada.

"OK, but those aren't actually feelings," Ryan said.

"OK. I guess I feel some tingling, tightness, tension in my stomach and my forearms," I offered.

"So you're stressed?" he asked.

"No, no, I don't get stressed," I objected.

Up to this point in my life, this idea of being "stressed" felt completely foreign to me, like an exotic disease that only someone who wasn't properly vaccinated could catch. Yes, I had suffered from existential anxiety, but I very rarely got worried or worked up in school over big exams or got nervous before big soccer games. As the pressures of entrepreneurial life picked up, I would label certain feelings as "super-focused" or maybe "concerned" (neither of which, you may note, are words that describe real *feelings).* The more rundown I got, the more poker-faced, impenetrable, and thick-skinned I became, with dulled sensitivities and little appreciation for much beyond "getting shit done."

Taking a different tack, he asked, "What are you afraid of?"

"I mean, fundamentally nothing," I insisted, as if trying to reassure a dubious investor. "But . . ."

He remained quiet, and suddenly a litany of fears burst from my mouth: that we were not moving fast enough and were going to miss our window to prove ourselves; that Dan and I would be held accountable if everything fell through; that I would be ridiculed as a failure; that I wasn't focused enough; that I was too focused; that I wasn't getting the support I needed; that I was somehow blocked from getting the support I really needed . . .

After purging all these feelings I'd tried to keep hidden in my shadow, Ryan taught me how to "formally" give them space. I would sit with this list and think to myself, *I include this in the realm of my experience. I accept and welcome my fears. Thank you for teaching me and showing me my edge. Without you I wouldn't be alive.*

Given that I was willing to work with my shadow in ceremonies, this practice made sense to me, and the realization that I could make space to acknowledge and work with my fears in my everyday life as well was extremely useful.

Ryan also taught me how to reassure myself that it would be OK even if my worst fears came true. *I'm breathing; I have food,* I would think. *If it tanks, it's OK. As long as I put myself on the line and do it with integrity, that's what matters.*

None of these practices made the fears disappear. In contrast, I went through waves of feeling *more* fearful because I wasn't ignoring them anymore. But I learned how to negotiate with my anxiety—to understand, acknowledge, and have a conscious relationship with it. Instead of trying to block out all my negative feelings, I realized that they were a part of taking on the challenge of building this company that I truly loved, even if I didn't always "like" it. When I stopped resisting this shadow side, I found it lost much of its power and, in turn, took on a power to proactively help me.

I can also testify that as I learned to be more transparent and honest with investors and potential investors about our specific struggles and where we'd been failing, it served to build *more* trust and stronger relationships.

And what of our dear guayusa? Could this amazing leaf have a shadow of its own? While this certainly should not dissuade anyone from loading up on cases of Runa, the answer is . . . of course, because it is alive.

Guayusa's MO is *¡Vamos!* (Let's do it!); although it has rich nuances and depths, its main deal is *Let's wake up and do this right.* As an entrepreneur, getting as much done as possible was exactly what I needed to do, which made guayusa an ideal ally. But at its extremes, *Let's go, let's go, let's go* can get militant, zealous, agitated, and harsh.

Unfortunately, leaning too heavily on any type of support, no matter how seemingly noble or "perfect" it might be, creates dependency or, worse, addiction. For me, learning to see the shadow of the very plant that I was working in service of, and that was supporting me to make it all happen in the first place, took a few years. By staying in a state of constant activity that bordered on mania, I was trying to repress the exhaustion and the despair that was under the surface. My ego didn't want to admit that I couldn't do it all myself. By running and gunning to such an extreme, I ended up firing bullets all over the place, including into my own foot.

After acknowledging the ways in which I had created over-dependency on guayusa, I started to cut back on my consumption, and decided not to drink it on the weekends to give my nervous system a break. Training my body to shift in and shift out of relationship to guayusa led me to a more conscious connection with the plant and a deeper appreciation for what it does to uplift me when I need it.

Of course, you might not drink three or four cans of Runa a day (if you do, thanks!), but almost everyone has developed their own crutches and aids. While I'm not saying to quit, it's worth the effort to step back, think about your relationship to these things, and determine whether you are using them to block out what your shadow might be trying to tell you. With conscious intention and redirection, thankfully you can reprogram them to serve more as tools than as weapons in disguise.

In addition to shifting your conscious relationship to whatever you depend on, look for counterbalances. To balance the stimulating power of guayusa, I began taking a range of "adaptogenic" herbs as complements. Adaptogens are a unique class of healing plants and natural substances that help the body adapt to stress and help restore and protect homeostasis. Research has shown certain adaptogens to recharge adrenal glands, which get readily taxed from stress and overstimulation. Reishi (a red mushroom used in Chinese medicine), Cordyceps (a fungus that lives on caterpillars in high mountain regions in China), shilajit (a mineral mass popular in Ayurvedic medicine in India), and ashwagandha (an herb also used in Ayurveda) are four adaptogens I've found immensely helpful to balance and regulate my system through periods of intense travel, stress, and overexertion.

How You Do Something Matters as Much as Why You Do It

In light of my World Tea Expo idiocy, I've come to realize that the *way* you conduct yourself in business is as important, if not more so, than the success of your stated mission. That means being mindful of how you treat people, acting with integrity and doing what you say you're going to do. You could make an esoteric argument about karmic repercussions, etc., etc., that justifies noble behavior, but it also just feels good. I feel lighter and freer when I'm being honest, transparent, and caring to those around me.

We've experienced extremes of supportive and malicious behavior throughout the growth of Runa. At one end, while we were still at Brown, I emailed a beverage industry consultant to see if she would chat with us. She said yes and spoke with Dan and me for about an hour. We thought it was just an informal chat with college students and we certainly never discussed money. I can't say we were super-stoked when she sent us a bill for $300 and then threatened to sue if we didn't pay.

On the opposite side, when we had to get our first New York warehouse space, we ended up contracting a small, family-owned company named Patrick Powers. They had an unornamented facility out on Long Island, packed with everything from caviar to boutonnieres. One doesn't expect that much from a warehouse except a safe, dry place to store things, but every time we dealt with them, they were upbeat, fun, appreciative of our business, and overly generous. They let us set up a place to pack custom samples free of charge, and when Caroline went out, they would drive her home to Brooklyn and wait until they saw she had gotten into her apartment. It made the whole experience feel great, and we loved doing business with them.

I have learned that you must have confidence in the hard work you're putting in, your mission, and your product. Your integrity will attract the right people without the need to resort to sleazy tactics, and if it doesn't, it wasn't meant to be. That lesson held true in Las Vegas at the World Tea Expo.

In the last hours of the convention, Tom Lisicki, the CEO of Stash Tea, came by our booth. Stash wasn't on our list of companies to attempt to harass via Facebook because they are the fifth-largest tea company in the U.S. and we assumed wouldn't be hip to guayusa. Tom fell in love with guayusa and we hit it off. He decided to come down to Ecuador with me shortly after and soon became our first big wholesale buyer, helping to deliver some of the revenues we so badly needed.

Chapter 9

Looking at Both Horizons

While it was great to have our tea boxes in stores, we always knew that the make-or-break proposition for Runa was going to be launching ready-to-drink beverages. To underscore why our "RTD" product was so important, the U.S. market for traditional hot tea is $2.6 billion a year. The market for bottled teas is more than double that, and rising. (The U.S. is something of a global anomaly, given that we are one of the only countries in the world that primarily consumes tea cold.)

Energy drinks are on another level. They've grown exponentially over the last fifteen years, and now constitute an astonishing $10.8 billion market in the U.S.—three times the size as when we first dreamed up Runa at Brown. So the path to more sales, we were sure, was through some sort of iced tea–energy drink products. We just didn't know how to get started.

As usual for Runa, the answer came from getting out and meeting people. We returned to Natural Products Expo East, the trade show we had basically snuck into when we were students at Brown. This time we had our own table, and performed our now standard routine of standing in the aisle and bursting at each passerby, "*Hi! Would you like to try some Amazonian tea?*" We got a reluctant "Sure, why not" from a skeptical-looking Englishman.

Our guayusa pot had been brewing for several hours at that point, and he suspiciously eyed the dark liquid in his cup before taking a sip. "Huh," he said. "I mean, how is it not bitter?"

We explained that overbrewing doesn't make guayusa bitter because it doesn't have the tannin levels of black or green tea.

"Have you guys ever thought about making a ready-to-drink version?" he asked.

It turned out we were speaking with Neil Kimberley, brand manager at Snapple during its runaway growth days in the 1990s and early 2000s. He'd then worked as a VP for Cadbury Schweppes. When we met him, he was between gigs before taking on a new role as head of global innovation for Hershey.

Our conversation continued beyond the trade show floor, and Neil eventually decided to jump on board as an investor, join our advisory board, and essentially teach us Beverage Industry 101 during long weekend talks in our conference room at 33 Flatbush Avenue.

Drawing on what we'd learned from giving out samples at Whole Foods, we distilled Runa's main proposition to "healthy energy," which was the hook that had grabbed the most people. From there we returned to the concept of "dramatic difference," thinking about what would set Runa apart from the dominant players in the energy drink category.

Our major inspiration was Vita Coco, which had passed $200 million in annual revenue (over $500 million nowadays) after only a handful of years in the market. The "What's in it for me?" for Vita Coco is that it rehydrates you after a workout or yoga session. That's the same promise that Gatorade makes, but Vita Coco is three times more expensive. Why the incredible demand?

We saw that Vita Coco had created a dramatic difference in the hydration-beverage category thanks to three key characteristics: (1) simple, (2) natural (3) functional.

First, it literally had one ingredient: water from a coconut. A bottle of Gatorade, by contrast, contains a long list of additives from high-fructose corn syrup to monopotassium phosphate.

Second, it came from nature. When Gatorade was introduced in 1965 after being concocted in a lab at the University of Florida, a big part of the appeal was that it was seen as "scientific." With the market swinging toward "natural" products, Vita Coco was able to offer the same benefit in a radically simple way, using taglines like "Our plant is a plant."

And third, it got the job done. Coconut water has high levels of magnesium and potassium and other mineral ions, making it clinically effective for rehydration.

Looking at the energy drink beverage category, we quickly realized that we had a parallel dramatic difference. Red Bull and Monster were the equivalent of Gatorade in the world of energy drinks, loaded with additives and oriented to the macho man, extreme mind-set.

Runa, on the other hand, offered sustained energy from a single leaf (simple) straight from the Amazon rainforest (natural), with a high level of caffeine and antioxidants that gave a more sustained energy experience (functional). We thought we could further distinguish ourselves by highlighting our social mission and avoiding the aggressive branding and marketing strategies that were the norm for the category.

If you're planning a new business venture of any kind, I really can't overemphasize how important it is to have a "dramatically" clear answer if someone asks: *What separates this product or service from everything else already on the market?* A few of my favorite examples of other young companies (all also started by entrepreneurs right out of college) with dramatically different products are: Exo bars, which makes protein bars using cricket protein; Back to the Roots, which produces grow-your-own mushroom kits from recycled coffee grounds; and Sir Kensington's, which is reviving the industry of ketchup and condiments with fantastic branding and the cleanest ingredients on the market.

Like these companies, our ongoing efforts to clearly define our "dramatic difference" have been vital to our success. If we were just another green tea or, even worse, another metallic-tasting, sugar-laden can of synthetic caffeine and chemicals, I'm sure we would have been dead in the water long ago.

The Wrong Kind of Explosive Growth

With much of the higher-level conceptual work done, there were still an incredible number of big decisions and tiny details to wrestle with before getting Runa product on store shelves.

We ultimately wanted to sell a carbonated "energy drink" type product in small cans to compete directly with Red Bull and Monster, but decided to launch with bottled iced teas to get our foot in the beverage door. Given the fundamental health appeal of the product itself, we felt safer opting to be perceived as a "tea" out of the gate. Next, we had to figure out what to put inside the bottles.

After some early tinkering, we befriended Eric Schnell, cofounder of Steaz, a line of organic green tea beverages and a pioneer in the natural foods industry. He fell in love with Runa, invested in the company, and offered to help us develop the flavors. He brought us to Allen Flavors, where together we came up with a plan to have flavors that would be accessible but with a twist. For example, since berry is a top-selling iced tea flavor, we gave it a slight twist and created "Hibiscus Berry."

We wanted our product to be lightly sweetened but not too sugary. The formulas with fifty calories per bottle tasted good to us and our officemates at 33 Flatbush, who we corralled to taste test for us. We decided that we would label sugar and calories as one serving per bottle as a way to take a stand for being transparent with customers, as it's really annoying when you buy a bottle of something and it's labeled as two servings: Who's going to drink the other half?

We found a design company in New York to work on the label. They struggled with the challenge of defining a visual landscape for this concept of healthy energy. The visual cues that commonly signify energy (lightning bolts, metallic colors, animalistic emblems, etc.) go pretty directly against traditional visual indications for health (muted colors, lots of white, simple layouts).

After flailing through a few rounds of designs, our planned

launch got closer and closer. With no designs that hit the mark, we settled on a "safe" option: white background, clean label, and big illustrations of the fruit flavors. It had the natural iced tea look we wanted, and might be mistaken for Honest Tea or Tazo. Dramatically different? No. But it looked nice enough, and we hoped that the quality of the product itself and story would carry it through.

In the beverage world, the vast majority of companies do not own their bottling operations, given the tens of millions of dollars it would take to build a facility. It proved to be surprisingly difficult to find the right third-party co-packer, since most only do huge production runs in the area of 500,000 bottles at one time. After some searching, we discovered a small operation in New Jersey that could do a run as small as 2,000 twelve-pack cases. Perfect!

Since our products were certified organic, we of course didn't want to add any artificial preservatives, which are used in traditional "cold fill" bottling operations (sodas, normal energy drinks, etc.) to keep the contents "shelf stable" so the finished product doesn't have to always be refrigerated. We chose to go with a "hot fill" process, which is one of essentially three ways you can bottle a beverage without preservatives and have it be shelf stable. Basically, it involves heating the bottles to around 200 degrees Fahrenheit just before filling them.

We'd hooked up with a New York area distributor, and the plan was to roll out Runa with an intense blitz in which our team would "ride-along" (as they say in the industry) with the distributor's sales reps to teach them about the product and help them sell it to accounts. We hired Alex Evans, my then girlfriend's sister's boyfriend, to be our New York sales manager—a towering, burly bear of a young man right out of college, with a bushy beard and a magnetic personality perfect for sales.

It was game time! After almost three and a half years of hustling in Ecuador and Brooklyn, our pipe dream had become a reality. Ever since I had started working with my coach, Ryan, he would say: "Visualize and feel yourself achieving the next big milestone for Runa." Invariably I would picture myself holding a bottle of Runa. Now it was real: we actually had bottles of Runa in our hands!

Within a few days of having our products on store shelves, strange reports began coming in that the bottles were, well, I guess the right term would be "spontaneously exploding." We began to investigate and found that, for some reason, the liquid in the bottles looked like it was fermenting. In the most extreme cases, that caused the caps to pop off, although mostly the product just tasted really rotten. The cases where nothing was visibly wrong with the drink were arguably the worst, because anyone who decided to try it for the first time would have simply thought the product wasn't good.

Very few times in my life (outside of a Shipibo ceremony) have I so suddenly gone from elation to confusion to steadily mounting despair. We mobilized everyone in the company, interns included, to go around and pull the entire run off the shelves. I still have terribly vivid memories of sitting for hours and hours at night with Alex Evans in a back alley in Bushwick, pouring out hundreds and hundreds of bottles of spoiled Runa from the back of my girlfriend's parents' now horrible-smelling minivan.

The most likely reason for the exploding bottles was that the bottler didn't handle the temperatures correctly during the hot fill process. However, when we went back to them, they said sheepishly, "You don't have any proof of that. We think your flavors were unstable . . ."

They were right about one thing: we had no proof, no way of figuring out what went wrong, and suing them wasn't worth it.

So we had to foot the bill and swallow the lost time. It was a nightmare I couldn't lucid-dream my way out of.

Read the Fine Print

It wasn't the only time that we got stuck holding the bag. Early on, we hired a web design company that required a large up-front payment. They ended up doing very little work on an extremely delayed timeline, and what they did do was quite mediocre. But there was no way for us to get the money back, given that we had set up the original contract so poorly. We had not included any safeguards to protect us in the event that their work was unacceptable. It was one of the first contracts we had ever signed in our lives, and we didn't even consider the possibility of the project not going spectacularly.

We also had ongoing headaches with the design company that did our first labels. The following year we hired a freelancer to make labels for some new unsweetened flavors we were adding to our line, because we didn't want to foot the bill for inflated agency costs just to create new fruit illustrations. The original design company soon reminded us that *they* actually owned the rights to the designs, meaning that we could use and modify them only with their contracted services. Shit.

They reminded us we had the option to execute something

called a "buyout fee" in the contract, so that we could purchase the designs and do whatever we wanted with them. You know, throw a few pennies their way for doing absolutely nothing beyond the hired work we paid them for in the first place. You know, like $50,000 worth of pennies . . .

The root of these issues is not only that we were inexperienced but that we were so eager to push ahead that we didn't check the details before committing to a course of action.

Sometimes, and relatively often in start-up scenarios, quick decision making is unavoidable. And the more intuitive shoot-from-the-hip strategy has at times worked quite well for us. We've had crazy amounts of seemingly magical support appear out of thin air.

But the times when making a quick decision was *actually* unavoidable were probably less than 50 percent of the times we *thought* it was unavoidable. Maybe even less than 15 percent of the time. Knowing when to be analytical and when to be intuitive is particularly challenging because the game is always changing.

In my view, modern society emphasizes analysis and rationality while devaluing our intuitive abilities, and that's a tragedy; it makes it difficult for people and companies to break out of the limitations they've inadvertently placed around themselves.

At the other extreme, some people adopt an overly "spiritual" approach that proposes the answer to every issue is to "just surrender" or "just trust it, man, it's all good." This approach only hands over the power of your agency and creative potential to some external other force. Having spiritual beliefs doesn't mean forfeiting the chance to act skillfully in a given situation.

In the Kichwa understanding of being *runa*, or "fully alive," one of the core aspects is that you access the full range of your human faculties in service of your goals, your prayers, and your intentions. In other words, you make use of every tool at your disposal, not just the handful at the front of your drawer. As they say, when you have a hammer, all your problems look like a nail.

When Amazonian healers treat patients with severe illnesses, they use the full range of tools at their disposal, and laugh at the idea of "isolating only one variable," as if arming a basketball team with only point guards were a good strategy. As a baseline, they prepare complex, highly crafted combinations of different plants with complex chemistry both to fight the disease and to support the body's overall immunity. From there, they prescribe specified dietary regimes to create the right conditions in the body for recovery. Beyond that, they use plant baths, plant poultices, vapors, and oils to support the physical body from the outside in. And they use a variety of spiritual tools, from singing, to meditation, to dream work, to look at and heal any deeper psycho-emotional or psycho-spiritual threads of the disease.

Parallel to my experience in business, the starting point has to be thorough research, analysis, calculation, and debate (within a team context). While, yes, there is inevitably some "magical" leap that must be made in a tough decision-making process, you have to first narrow the gap as much as possible. Nothing can substitute for it. Google CEO Larry Page says "I've learned that your intuition about things you don't know that much about isn't very good."

Especially in the world of fast-moving entrepreneurship, it's critical to resist the seductive tendency to think you have to act *now* and to overvalue "gut decisions." Get multiple bids on a project, run downside scenarios of a potential idea, and if for some reason you don't, make sure you have a very good reason for skipping ahead.

One specific technique I've seen to be immensely powerful in helping add additional rigor to hiring and partnership decisions in particular is to do "backdoor reference checks." If you are hiring someone or looking to work with a contractor, never just call the people they list as references—who, of course, are handpicked because they will say nice things. Take the time to find other people the candidate has worked with and call them; in other words, go through the back door. Sometimes this can mean just cold-calling a company they used to work for and asking to speak with someone who used to work with them. This will give you a much more honest read on their abilities and what it will be like to work with them. It takes more time and effort, but it can save you from untold problems down the line.

After all the analysis has been done, a decision still must be made. In difficult relationship situations or when charting new territory on the business front, it's rare to have enough information where the decision is cut-and-dried. Like the Amazon itself, difficult situations are usually "serpentine and moist," requiring the permeable, mutable power of your intuitive faculties to *feel* into it. (Yes, I did just recommend "feeling" as an effective tool for making "business" decisions. I know it sounds "out there," but it works.)

In order to feel comfortable trusting my intuitive read on a situation, "clearing my filters" is an important preparatory step. While sometimes this involves a vision quest or a plant *dieta*, I've found a range of more accessible practices I can use on a daily basis when needed.

For example, I will spend thirty minutes before going to bed journaling about a particular challenge I'm having, and then I will consciously focus on that challenge before falling asleep. The following morning I write down my dreams as soon as I wake up, and then journal for another fifteen to twenty minutes about the dream and whatever else comes to mind.

At first I almost always think, *Well, that dream was completely meaningless and random*. Then, after fifteen minutes of sitting with it and just writing in a stream of consciousness, I get to a "holy shit" moment. It doesn't take any specialized dream interpretation techniques or symbolism; just take the time to feel what comes up and reflect upon it.

I've also found value in a range of archaic methodologies for tapping into deeper, subtler layers of a situation when looking for guidance. From coca leaf readings (similar to tea leaf readings in Asia) to the *I Ching* (the ancient Chinese book of divination) to tarot cards, I've come to appreciate the way these tools help me see the effects of how my approach, mind-set, and underlying motivations are impacting the situation at hand.

The inner workings of why and how these techniques might work is beyond me. Personally, I'm open to both the more accessible perspective that they are effective because they speak in the language of the subconscious mind through metaphor (similar to a basic understanding of dream interpretation) and also the more esoteric one: that they possess the ability to enlist the help and guidance of unseen allies and/or spirits.

Rather than going to some third party who has some special power to interpret the coca leaves or an *I Ching* throw, the key for me is to push myself to use these tools myself and challenge my own ability to find useful reflections in what they are saying. I never use them to look for definite answers or try to "see the future" but purely to get a deeper sense of how to act with the most alignment in any given situation.

Attracting New Layers of Support

This openness to what would not really be considered "traditional" ways of doing business certainly helped in concrete ways as we began to garner material support (i.e., money) from sources we never considered.

Maria Jose, who had run the grant program that gave us our first seed money for our R & D facility, had moved over to the ministry of production, where she'd been tasked with creating a first-of-its-kind impact-investing program.

The idea was for the Ecuadorian government to make direct equity investments in early-stage private companies that were creating jobs and social impact in the country. The government would initially buy shares in the companies and then over time sell their shares to the employees and farmers that the companies benefit—an interesting use of capitalist tactics to support socialist goals. Maria Jose, who had worked with us on the earlier grant we'd received from the Ecuadorian government, called to let me know that they wanted us to apply, showing that when you do right by your partners you never know what goodwill might come back to you later.

We saw it as an amazing though potentially complicated way to get growth capital, build a real factory, and, over time, make the farmers owners of the company with us. After months and months of applications, reviews, interviews, and so on, we were one of three companies out of seven hundred applicants chosen to receive a $500,000 investment from the ministry.

As we negotiated the final agreement, we caught a few clauses in the contract at the eleventh hour that wouldn't give us enough flexibility in our growth strategy, but the government said it was too late to change and we had to take it or leave it. Having learned our lessons from our previous contract fiascos, Francisco and I made the tough decision to walk away, but two weeks later they called us back, agreed to our revised terms, and signed the deal. That made them minority shareholders in Runa's Ecuadorian company, with our U.S. company, Runa LLC, retaining the majority stake.

A major break came for Runa Foundation shortly after. I'd recently become friends with Chris, a tea industry expert in New York who fell in love with guayusa and wanted to see our production line for himself. He joined me for one of my blitz trips to Ecuador for a long weekend of work and loved every second of the whirlwind tour.

He called me a few days later and said, "Hey, I had dinner with my uncle last night, told him about the trip, and he's very interested in what you're doing and wants to meet with you."

Chris's uncle just happened to be a billionaire with a passion for environmental sustainability. "The meeting will be short," Chris warned. "He doesn't like to waste time and he's a very intuitive guy. He'll either like you or he won't."

I met his uncle on the floor of the warehouse where a new company he had just invested in was setting up shop. Taking a quick break from his meetings, we sat in folding chairs amid pallets upon pallets of products stacked thirty feet high. Around eighty years old, he looked quite a bit like my grandfather at that age, carrying himself with a thoughtful sincerity and almost childlike glow.

The conversation mostly consisted of me telling him about Runa, Runa Foundation, and where I thought it was all going. He listened intently and said little. After no more than fifteen minutes he smiled and looked intently at me. "OK," he said simply. "I'm going to send you a check for $500,000 as a donation to the Runa Foundation."

He then reached out to shake my hand as a farewell. As Chris walked me out, I did a string of "reality test" exercises to make sure I wasn't actually dreaming.

By that point I'd done enough fundraising to know that you should never count on any commitments until the money is actually in your bank account. Five days later, we opened the mail and saw a check for half a million dollars made out to the Runa Foundation.

After the exploding-bottle fiasco, our advisors Tim Sullivan and Neil Kimberley pulled out all the stops and managed to get us into a new bottler relatively quickly (a Coca-Cola–approved facility that almost never takes on small customers). We got the bottles into some big accounts, including Whole Foods and Wegmans, and spent the summer doing our usual nonstop sampling at every account that we could. Despite the horrible start to our bottled line in the summer of 2012, we somehow managed to get back on track and broke $1 million in sales that year.

Back when that number sounded like an impossible fantasy, Dan and I had agreed that we would get guayusa leaf tattoos once we achieved the goal. So after work one day we went up to Williamsburg in Brooklyn to get bright green guayusa leaves inked on our skin by my incredibly talented friend Amy Shapiro.

I've since tried to convince our CFO to get a guayusa leaf teardrop tattoo under her eye when we break $100 million, but so far she has not agreed.

Chapter 10

Hijack Your Resistance

During the first few years of Runa, my pursuit of more in-depth shamanic studies was temporarily shelved. The first big blow happened when Herlinda died of uterine cancer. On top of that, studying anything outside the basics needed to help Runa survive, let alone thrive, just wasn't in the cards. Although guayusa and tobacco helped keep me on the rails (mostly), my connection to these plants became more about maintenance than cultivation.

My last *dieta* in Peru during college felt like it somehow set me off on the task of building Runa. The deep sense of responsibility I felt for creating Runa as a vehicle for guayusa to reach the modern world, as a sort of ambassador for the broader Amazonian traditions, was all-consuming. The years of unpacking the vision and translating shamanic principles into a real-life business were utterly exhausting, and I started to feel like the tattered bandages on my battle wounds were wearing thin.

But with Runa getting some solid footing and growing to new levels, I felt a fresh need to anchor down further into my spiritual practice for new energy and inspiration. I met a guy who raved about these two Shipibo shamans he had been working with in Peru, and for some reason I felt a warmth in my heart every time he mentioned them. So in 2014 I forced myself to take ten days off from work and went to Peru to meet them.

Julio was in his seventies, usually reserved but spritely when he opened up. His entire life had been spent doing dietas with a tremendous number of plants, including many that are extremely powerful but also potentially fatal if taken in the wrong doses. His nephew Arturo was thirty but looked like he was sixteen. He had a lightness and softness to him that came out in the open affection he showed his wife and kids. His father, a powerful *meraya* (master Shipibo shaman), had put Arturo on his first training diet at age eight, when he spent six months on dieta with three powerful plants, spending days by himself in the jungle, eating one meal a day. When Arturo's father died around a decade later, he continued his training with Julio.

During our first of many ceremonies, I had an unshakable feeling of familiarity with Arturo in particular and felt very welcomed by him.

They suggested that I start an eight-week *dieta* with *bobinsana*, as it's commonly called in Peru (*semein* in Shipibo), a small tree that grows near rivers and streams in the Amazon and produces magnificent pink and white flowers. It is also known for having an incredibly sophisticated, far-reaching root system, so that the trees can grow fully horizontal and even downward from the side of a steep bank. The Shipibo say that it is a master of the water element, aligned with the spirit of the pink river dolphins in the Amazon, and a profound teacher.

He didn't explain why he recommended *bobinsana* specifically, but after several years scrambling to get Runa up and running, I was ready to find some grounding and dig some deeper roots.

"Tating Channing?"

After two weeks in Peru, I came back to Brooklyn to finish the *dieta*, consuming a strong decoction of boiled *bobinsana* root extract on a daily basis and doing my best to juggle work responsibilities at the same time. In the meantime, I followed the usual *dieta* restrictions: no sex, no spices, etc.

I felt a spark come back into my life. During my dreams and meditations, I could feel the *bobinsana* weaving itself into my nervous system and resurfacing unprocessed fragments of different sicknesses, stresses, and confusions that I had gotten past *just* enough to continue on with my grind and get back up to "normal" speed but not fully resolve. Every night I had dreams of incredible waterfalls, underwater caves and palaces, and exploding dams of water that would flood the Runa office or a home I was living in. A few times I woke up in the middle of the night and ran to the bathroom to puke. Doing *dietas* while not in isolation isn't recommended at all. I had no other way to do it at the time, but I've moved away from doing such "socialized" *dietas*, given the risks.

Shortly after I got back from Peru, I went up on a Saturday

to Greenwich, Connecticut, to meet with one of our investors, Sanjay, an older Indian gentleman I'd been introduced to by Neil Kimberley, the Englishman who had helped us come up with our bottled product. He and Sanjay had met through a Greenwich cricket club for British and Commonwealth expatriates.

As we sat on a park bench and chatted, Sanjay ran through his mental Rolodex, searching for people who might be interested in Runa, and landed on a name.

"Do you know who 'Tating Channing' is?" he asked earnestly.

"Um, I think you mean 'Channing Tatum,'" I ventured. "Yeah . . . yeah, I know who that is."

"Oh, great! Do you think he could be helpful to your company?"

Yes, I told Sanjay, a connection with Channing Tatum could certainly be valuable.

Sanjay connected me to his good friend Neil Grayson, a mind-blowing painter in TriBeCa who was friends with Channing and his business partner, Reid Carolin. Neil called Reid soon after to tell him that they needed to check out this drink called Runa, to which Reid responded, "Runa? We live on Runa."

It turned out Channing and Reid had discovered it at Whole Foods when they were scripting *Magic Mike* and consumed numerous bottles and cans of Runa every day (and night) while they were on deadline to write the whole script in just a few weeks.

Encouraged, Neil sent Reid and Channing our brand overview presentation, to which Channing wrote back "Haha. Nice try, Neil." Confused, Neil called him to ask what he thought was a joke.

"Really, Neil? Tyler Gage? You could have tried something less obvious," Channing said.

That jolted Neil to remember that Tyler Gage had been the exact name of Channing's character in the 2006 movie *Step Up*, the breakout film that had helped launch his career. "Tyler Gage" sounded too obvious to not be a gag.

On my side, I had been getting jokes directed at me since the movie came out, so I was intimately aware of the connection. My go-to response had been to tell people that I was the inspiration behind the movie because the producers saw me tearing up the dance clubs in San Francisco when I was a teenager.

In actuality, celebrity and pop culture had been generally far away from my Amazonian-plant–obsessed reality. I was so detached that my friends often mocked me for my lack of familiarity with cultural icons and public figures.

After Neil reassured Channing that there is indeed a *real* Tyler Gage who *really* is the cofounder of this Amazonian tea company, Channing and Reid felt like they had no choice but to take the meeting.

Channing was filming *21 Jump Street* in New Orleans and invited Sanjay, Neil, and me to fly down that weekend. Though I was in the middle of my *bobinsana dieta* and New Orleans, with its many temtpations, is up there on the list of non-*dieta*-friendly places in the country, I figured I would have to find a way.

We stopped by Saints & Sinners, the bar and restaurant

Channing owns on Bourbon Street, and then settled at a restaurant for dinner. The prior days I'd been consumed with how I could navigate the situation without immediately announcing, "Hey guys, I'm a total whack job and can't drink, let alone eat salt right now, because I'm on a weird shamanic plant *dieta* thing . . . So let's just overlook that and talk business, cool?"

After sitting down and ordering food, I excused myself to "go to the bathroom" so that I could corner the waiter and explain that I had some very severe allergies and needed the chicken and potatoes I had ordered to come absolutely plain.

Reid, Channing, and I hit it off immediately, recognizing that we all had proclivities for extreme adventures and intense training. As the conversation transitioned to Runa, Reid kicked it off, simply saying, "We love the product, but I'm curious: How much would you want us involved?"

I hesitated a moment. Obviously, I didn't want to blow my chance to create a partnership with these guys. Deep down, I really wanted them to be genuinely involved with the company and help in a million ways, but I was scared of seeming desperate and overeager.

The easy alternative, I knew, would be to just ask for an investment and social media support, and call it a day. But would that actually help at all? And would they want me to pay them to do stuff for us? That didn't feel right, and we didn't have money for that anyway.

Rather than bow down to these fears, something rose up inside me, and I decided to hijack my resistance and ride it like a wave.

"I don't want an endorsement," I began, "You guys are professional storytellers, and the essence of what we are doing is trying to tell a powerful story. We're trying to tell the story of this crazy leaf and build a community around that. Honestly, we could use help figuring out how to get the depth and richness of that story out to more people. It's been hard. We'd love to have you involved as much as possible and figure out what that looks like together. I can't say I have a clear idea right now . . ."

To which I got a head nod from Reid and a simple "Word" from Channing, and then quickly another question about whether we were contemplating any new products. *Shit, was that the right answer?* I wondered. The rest of the dinner seemed to go great, and Reid said he would call me the next day with some feedback as we said good-bye outside the restaurant.

As I waited at the airport the next morning, Reid called. "We were worried you were just some kind of business schmuck and just wanted an endorsement," he said. "We loved your honesty, your passion, and we're excited by the challenge of getting this story out in the world. We'd like to invest in the business. We don't want any payment or BS like that. The only thing is that we want to come to Ecuador."

Four months later, Channing, Reid, Neil, Dan, and I were sitting with Virgilio's family for a sunrise guayusa ceremony in Napo, on the banks of the resplendent Hollín River. I'd been coming to this spot for years with Virgilio's family, watching the mist break in the morning light, but had never anticipated this scene.

I remembered the very first ceremony Dan and I had with

Alejandro and his family just a few years back, and saw the same bright-eyed wonder in Reid's and Channing's faces as Virgilio passionately told Kichwa hunting myths while his wife poured us gourd after gourd of strongly brewed guayusa.

As the ceremony ended, Channing headed up to the top of the bridge nearby, forty feet above the rushing water below. He threw a perfect backflip and almost got swept downriver by the current after landing. In between adventures, Reid and Channing worked on the script for *Magic Mike XXL*.

We each brought a friend along for the ride. Andy Isaacson, a fellow Brown grad and friend of ours from Brooklyn, joined us to write a feature article for *Men's Fitness*. Reid and Channing brought Brian Bowen Smith, a celebrity photographer (and also a former professional skater and total madman) they had known for years.

On the way back to Archidona after a breakfast of fresh eggs cooked on the fire with just-harvested heart of palm in a banana-leaf wrap, we stopped by the home and family farm of Ruth Grefa. Ruth was one of the leaders in the Kichwa community of San José. Ever since my early days in Ecuador, I'd spent time with Ruth and the other women leaders of San José, who proudly run their community. Sitting with them in the blazing sun as they made traditional Kichwa bracelets and necklaces, rarely would more than five minutes pass without one of the women cracking a joke, often some sexual innuendo (as Kichwa humor tends to be), leading the whole flock to burst out in shrieks and hoots.

Their many kids intermittently huddled at their knees,

chased and tickled each other, and played with a pet *cuchocho*, a miniature relative of the raccoon with small ears and a slightly upturned nose. They are so cute and defenseless that their entire evolutionary strategy must have been to make themselves uncontrollably adorable to humans and seek refuge in their homes.

Ruth and her friends were one of the very first groups to plant a community guayusa nursery, back in 2010. Virgilio, Oscar, and I would visit on weekends with our interns to harvest small cuttings and plant them in a rustic nursery we built together with them. There was no budget for any materials, and none requested—just a simple, shared recognition that this was important for the community, even though where exactly it was leading was unclear at the time. These women were going to do this as they had done everything for centuries: by working together, laughing, and using whatever resources they had on hand.

Now five years later, we toured Ruth's *chakra* with more than three hundred guayusa trees standing over our heads, flush with richly green leaves that grew bigger than our hands. The trees flourished in her abundant forest garden next to dozens of other unique fruit and medicinal plant species.

Over the last few years guayusa has become Ruth's most profitable crop, earning her almost twice as much income as her next most profitable crop, organic cacao beans used to make chocolate. She's used the additional income to pay for the education of her son and her daughter, Wiñay and María, in addition to becoming an entrepreneur herself and starting a small store that stocks basic household items and school supplies.

That night we brought the guys along for our annual company tradition: white-water rafting . . . at midnight. Since most of our thirty full-time team members in Ecuador were local Kichwa people who actually know the dangers of the river, the general consensus was that such a proposition was purely idiotic. With a lot of guayusa and a bit of rum the sentiment usually changed.

In addition to navigating the class 3 rapids of the Jatunyaku River, most of the trip was spent with one boat attacking another, trying to throw the entire crew overboard into the cold water that flows from the Andes. As we took a break on the shore halfway down, a lightning storm rolled overhead, lighting up the jungle with brilliant flashes. Thankfully it veered south and allowed us to finish the trip, but it continued to offer streaks of illumination as we shivered our way to the end.

After the factory tour the next day, we couldn't leave Archidona without getting in a game of "Ecuavoley," which is the most popular sport in Ecuador, even beyond soccer. A twisted kind of three-on-three volleyball, Ecuavoley allows you to *almost* catch and throw the ball (not actually, but to a degree that would definitely be in violation of normal volleyball rules). It is played with a very high net, making the goal to strategically deceive the other team and flick the ball into the small corners where the other team's defense isn't.

Channing, Reid, and I teamed up against some Kichwa guys from the neighborhood where Runa Foundation had a house for interns. From all appearances, it would have seemed that the advantage went to us gringos: I'd played soccer in college, Reid had played hockey, and Channing had played football. In addition, Reid is about six foot six and our tallest opponent was maybe five foot eight at best.

But even with Reid's ability to spike—which garnered

profound amusement from the dozens of locals who flocked around—the Ecuadorians schooled us with their tactical ball placement. I didn't quite understand how competitive Reid and Channing were until I saw them diving all around the dirt court, trying save the shots the Ecuadorians were dropping around us, getting legitimately agitated in the process. These guys *hated* to lose as much as I did!

Ecuadorians know Channing from action movies such as *White House Down* and *G.I. Joe: The Rise of Cobra*, and the crowd loved seeing the guy they'd watched on long bus trips get worked over, bloody, and frustrated on their local court. When our public embarrassment was finally over, we all hung out drinking beers and guayusa with the neighborhood.

Go Sit in the Forest. Listen.

I wanted to make Channing and Reid's trip especially memorable, and take advantage of the opportunity to explore a bit myself. My good friends Oliver Utne and Belen Paez had told me for years about a tribe called the Sápara, a group of only five hundred remaining members who live deep in the jungle. Oliver and Belen had extended an open invitation to join them on a trip, so I took them up on the offer.

We took a few tiny prop planes out over hundreds of miles of pristine jungle and landed on an airstrip that had been cleared by machete. The entire community of Llanchamacocha eagerly awaited our arrival with radiant smiles and hugs. Manari Ushigua, the leader of the community, was around forty-five years old, with long black hair and a joyous earnestness about him.

"You are coming in as part of our community. We don't believe in the concept of 'tourists,'" he said. "We welcome you into our ways, but first we need to cleanse you of whatever you're bringing in."

They led us to the river and asked us to sit in it quietly and just listen and feel. From there, they brought us to a big clay pot that was filled with plants. They dipped gourds and poured the water over us. They then blew tobacco smoke over our bodies and had us snort a very strong brew of ground tobacco leaves. Assuming most people reading this have never snorted tobacco juice, it's sort of like putting an electrical live wire into your brain and sinuses.

Once cleansed, Manari and his brothers led us on a hike in the jungle, during which they introduced us to dozens of medicinal plants. We drank water from freshly cut vines and ate fruits they climbed thirty-foot trees to harvest.

As they explained various plants to us, one of Manari's brothers showed us one they used to cure snakebites. When I asked if he had ever been bitten, he nonchalantly nodded and responded, "*Sí.*"

Sensing more to the story, I asked how many times he'd been bitten.

"*Nueve,*" he said. (Yes, nine times!)

As I was pondering getting attacked by highly poisonous vipers nine times, he added that their mother had been bitten fifteen times and that no one in the memory of their tribe had died of a snakebite. They had a refined repertoire of plants they use internally and topically to cure what would otherwise be lethal snakebites, in the same way we might treat a common cold with Robitussin.

That was good to know, because at the end of our walk we were each left to sit alone in the jungle for half an hour just to absorb the sounds and atmosphere. Simply knowing that the trilling of each insect and the cooing of each bird were identifiable to Manari and his family gave the space a sense of intimacy and wonder.

I absolutely loved the simplicity and reverence for nature that permeated the Sápara culture. The neighboring tribes around them are traditionally bold warriors and fierce in their ways, while for whatever reason the Sápara have a serenity at the heart of their people, a glowing stoicism that is truly their own. Whereas Shipibo medicine is extremely clinical and complex, the Sápara have a deep respect for the simple power of nature and the medicine woven into their rainforest home. Their main prescriptions? Go sit in the river. Go sit in the forest. Listen.

Whereas the master plant of the Amazonian Kichwa people is guayusa—it's considered their main teacher and portal between the human and natural worlds—the Sápara revere *chiricaspi* (botanical name *Brunfelsia grandiflora*), a dense shrub with beautiful royal-purple flowers (although they can also be white). It definitely makes the shortlist of most commonly used shamanic plants across cultures in the Amazon. In Peru, where it's known as *chiric sanango*, you can find shamans who specialize in the use of the plant and others like it; they're known as *sanangueros*.

Because *chiricaspi* causes chills and tingling when consumed, it's known as the "tree of chills" and is used medicinally to treat "heat-inducing" illnesses such as fever, diarrhea, wounds, and inflammations.

The Sápara employ *chiricaspi* for much more. Manari told us they believe the plant has roots in the world of dreams and that "it carries the electricity of cosmic love from the heart of the universe" and "it teaches you how to aim" (in hunting and in life).

We learned that, much like the Amazonian Kichwa, the Sápara revered dreams and dream interpretation. Manari's dad had been a powerful shaman and had eleven kids, and it was said he had passed to each of them one part of his particularly large shamanic toolkit. Manari had received his gift for decoding dreams.

Before going to bed on our first night in the village, as we each lay on plantain leaves around a fire, staring up at streams of bright stars, Manari squeezed juice from a pile of *chiricaspi* leaves directly into our mouths.

At sunrise we awoke, drank guayusa, jumped in the river, and had another round of plant baths. When we gathered to discuss our dreams with Manari, Brian started. "I don't know," he said. "Everything seems normal. I mean, it's beautiful here, I feel good . . ." And then he began bawling. "Oh, huh, wow, I guess there is more going on than meets the eye! This is just such a powerful experience, I guess I don't even know how to process it. I'm just . . . really thankful for life."

Channing said that after he went to sleep, an elderly indigenous man had come to him in a dream and guided him through the Sápara cosmology and myths the entire night. "It was pretty mind-bending and intense."

Manari listened and said, "That was my father, showing you the history and spirit of my people and making sure you know that you're very welcome here."

Later that day, as part of the cross-cultural experience, the community played some music and showed us a traditional dance in the main community hut. They then asked us if we knew how to dance, so we all stared at Channing, who nodded and asked Brian to beatbox. I think it's safe to say that the Sápara had never seen anyone break-dance before. Brian started to throw backflips, and the Sápara women were on the ground crying from laughing so hard.

One part of the trip that we didn't particularly enjoy was drinking *chicha*, which is a slightly alcoholic drink the women make by boiling manioc root and then chewing and spitting it back into a pot to let it ferment. It *is* nourishing and probiotic, but the taste, oh, the taste . . . imagine a cross of potatoes, spoiled milk, and kombucha. It is a core staple of Amazonian culture, and it's considered extremely rude not to consume it if offered. Our usual method of dealing with it was to smile, put the bowl to our lips, pretend to drink, and then pass it to the next person.

On our last day, several Sápara women asked us if we wanted to play a game. We excitedly agreed. "OK, first, you guys start clucking like chickens," they said.

We all went for it without reserve, clucking around like old hens, bobbing our heads, and loving it. As we cooed and flapped, several women reached into the bottom of the *chicha* pot and grabbed handfuls of sludge. They walked over to each one of us, grabbed the backs of our heads, opened our mouths, and shoved the fistfuls of white goop into our mouths, cackling and saying "Eat, baby bird!"

While hysterically laughing at how badly they had gotten us and choking at the same time, I managed to spit out the chunks before swallowing them and saw Channing doing the same next to me. As I looked down the line, Dan and Reid were staring at me with uncomfortably intense gazes, and Reid stuttered, "You guys swallowed it, r-r-r-right?"

My eyes widened and I shook my head disapprovingly. Both bolted off into the jungle and started puking, followed by continued laughter from the community.

Bad weather delayed our flight out of the jungle, and then our van broke down on the drive back to Quito. We arrived less than an hour before our flight was supposed to leave for the U.S., and Channing had to get back for a *Vanity Fair* cover shoot with Annie Leibovitz the following morning.

As we pulled up to the airport we saw at least a hundred people gathered outside with big signs. We thought it was a protest and my nerves tightened even further. But somehow the word got out that Channing was about to fly out, and the crowd was a mob of fans.

I ran inside and, as I feared, the Avianca airline desk was closed and deserted, lights off. Interrogating an airport employee nearby, I learned the airline had an office in a separate tower on the other side of the airport that *might* have some people still in it.

I sprinted back to the car, asked the rest of the guys to wait, and told Channing to follow me. We tore across the airport, through a propped open security door, up five flights of stairs, and somehow found the Avianca office, staffed by three twenty-five-year-old Ecuadorian women sitting at computers.

Their eyes widened in shock when they saw who had just come in. I didn't need to say much before they were dashing back with us to the Avianca counter, where they reopened the check-in system and called a security escort. As soon as Channing got his boarding pass, he left us to finish check-in and ran back to the crowd who had been waiting for him to sign autographs and have some pictures taken.

Finally, we rushed through the airport and got on the flight with no time to spare. When we landed, Channing reflected to me that the trip fit his criteria for a successful adventure. His definition of such paralleled a piece of acting advice he said he learned early in his career and had been his guiding star: "If you're not terrified that you're about to fail completely, then you're not doing it right."

Chapter 11

Unwinding, Unraveling as the Ancestors Say

All of 2014 continued at the pace we'd set running through the airport in Quito.

During the summer of 2013, we'd finally launched our line of carbonated "clean energy drink" cans in New York City, with a provocative, but minimally successful marketing campaign with hundreds of posters across the city. In the pictures on the posters, I had dressed up to look like a tweaked-out candy raver and Dan as a coked-out banker with the tagline "Clean Up Your Energy" at the bottom.

Although the campaign didn't rally as much attention as we had hoped, the product started to sell. After the turn of the new year, the line was accepted into almost all Whole Foods and Safeway stores across the country, growing our "doors" by almost 1,500. We then hired our first real executive in the U.S., Sara Perkins as our CFO, to keep up with the growth.

National Geographic and *Fast Company* produced major features on us, and Channing went on Jimmy Fallon and talked extensively about our trip to Ecuador, adding a great line that drinking Runa gives him "the energy of the gods."

Because we invested heavily in sales and marketing support, we burned through our last round of investment and were back in fundraising mode yet again. Our stress levels rose, perhaps even higher than before, since Dan and I had naïvely thought we were through the toughest part. Now it hit us that we were just getting started and we would absolutely need the energy of the gods to get through the challenges ahead.

Of course, the biggest strain on both of us was the continual hunt for investors. We needed a big injection of cash to fund our expansion, and I was chasing every lead I had to try to get a deal done ASAP.

One negotiation was with a traditional venture capital firm that offered $6 million for a minority stake in Runa. When we read the fine print, however, we saw that the contract included a number of aggressive terms, all the way up to the possibility that the venture capitalists could take control of the company if we didn't accomplish our sales goals. After discussing it with our lawyer and each other, we decided to walk away.

Another potential deal with a wealthy family fell through when they pulled out at the very last minute, fearing that the risks of working in Ecuador were too high.

By that point we were scrambling to keep the doors open, our list of payables stacking up into the hundreds of thousands as the weeks went by. Dan, Sara, and I stopped paying ourselves. We avoided phone calls from angry vendors we owed money to, trying to buy us some time to raise the funds to pay them.

After a few more months of negotiations and intensive due diligence, we closed $8 million in funding from a group of investors including family offices, "impact investors" (investment funds that seek to create social good in addition to their returns), and beverage industry angel investors. Yet again, the failure of our ambitions of "going big" and getting a major venture capital investment led us back to our roots of collaboration and finding strength in diversity. This "club deal"—what it's called when multiple investors join together in a round—gave us more connections, more support, and even more capital than we originally set out to raise.

The day the investments cleared our bank account, we popped champagne bottles in the office and started writing checks to the long list of people we owed money.

Little did we know we were in for a ride much like the effects of the champagne we chugged. Celebratory vibe? Check. Tastes great? Check. Feel shitty when you wake up the next morning? That too.

Looked at one way, the investment was the big gulp of medicine that saved the company. But I should have remembered Arturo's caution that "when you ask for medicine, the shadow comes first."

I wasn't the slightest bit prepared.

The Shadow Returns

For years at that point, as I'm sure is obvious, I'd been in an uber-hustling, go-go-go, entrepreneur mode. Yes, I'd worked at toning down some of my anxiety and rougher edges, but my basic mode of existence was a constant thrum of *Get moving, you have to make this work!*

I was so immersed in that state that I didn't even realize there could be any other way to run a business. Sara, our CFO, was a godsend, implementing financial and operating procedures that were critical in keeping us on the rails, but I continued to pursue every opportunity I could. I knew that not everything was going to work, so if I only pursued three options, we might be left with nothing. But if I tried thirty different things, one or two might click and we would survive.

One particular opportunity that had shown increasing promise was a "private label" deal with one of the biggest supermarket chains in the country. Their proposal was that Runa would bottle our drinks but place their store brand label on it instead of Runa's; they would then market and sell the product exclusively in their stores. I estimated the arrangement to be worth several hundred thousand dollars per year of profit for us. I thought it would be a great way to sell more guayusa through a creative format, generating more income for the farmers and more awareness of the ingredient.

I had negotiated the deal down to the finish line by the time I brought it to anyone else. Since I was constantly pursuing dozens and dozens of different leads at any one time, all of which had varying degrees of probability and potential, I'd come to see that one of the hardest parts of my job was deciding exactly when to communicate something to my team and the board. If I presented an opportunity too soon, I wouldn't be prepared to face the intense scrutiny of our team, who would be skeptical given the still-amorphous nature of the proposal. If I waited too long, however, people were immediately critical that I hadn't brought the opportunity to their attention sooner and worried that they couldn't still influence the outcome.

Although Dan knew I was working on the private label deal, he hated it once he heard the details. In addition to other concerns, he didn't think the products would sell as well as they projected and, rather than making any profit, we would end up in the hole.

In short, we came to a total impasse over it. Historically, if we disagreed on something, we brought it to our advisors and tended to go with their counsel. This time, however, their opinions were as mixed as ours: some thought it was a good deal, others cautioned against it. I found that it was becoming harder to rely on our mentors, because the questions we had were increasingly nuanced, requiring more time and analysis than a simple phone conversation would allow.

Without clear agreement from our team, we presented both sides to our board of directors, which we had recently formed after the latest round of investment. The truth was that I had already spent so much time working on the deal and pushed the private label conversation so far that I had become emotionally invested. But I feared that if I told the board that I had already overcommitted us, they would just pull the plug immediately and it would make me look bad.

There wasn't much enthusiasm about the deal, but I pushed so hard that I convinced the majority of the board to very reluctantly let me go ahead with it. I felt triumphant, and doggedly marched forward to put the pieces in place.

In the meantime, we'd had a couple of tough quarters overall, with margins substantially lower than we'd projected. Business was growing faster than we had expected on the West Coast, but since we didn't have a bottling facility there yet, we were shipping small quantities from our East Coast bottler, inflating our freight costs beyond belief. We were growing at more than 80 percent year over year at that point, but we had aggressively projected growth rates of almost double that to our new investors. Needless to say, they weren't pleased.

Increasingly critical and suspicious, they asked more and more questions. While the upside to taking an investment from "mission-aligned" investors was that they appreciated the "triple bottom line" approach we had to business (financial, social, and environmental), the challenge was that they had limited to no experience in the beverage industry.

Dan, Sara, and I felt they were asking the wrong questions and didn't have the basic experience required to understand the variables and interwoven levers that would determine the success or failure of our business. As they began to understand this concept, their response was to ask us to hire expensive consultants to do a "deep dive" on the business. While the willingness to really understand our business is exactly what we asked for, I found the concept of wasting our time and precious new cash on cocky consultants with high price tags to be pretty offensive. *We* were the scrappy entrepreneurs who had been breaking convention, *we* were smarter than these old-school beverage people anyhow, and *we* were the ones who were going to make it work, I thought as I fumed around the office late at night.

I started to feel a knot in my stomach every time I spoke with the board. At first I tried a deferential "Sure, thank you for all the generous help" tone, but my attempts at being accommodating only fueled my increasingly pent-up anger at the lack of support I felt.

I vividly remember a phone conversation we had on Christmas Day when comments like "Please accept that we have a lot more business experience than you" were met by "How about you 'please accept' that you haven't *actually* taken the time to understand our business?" That was met with "Well, then what we want to *very nicely stress* is that our closer involvement is not an option to debate or negotiate. You don't have a say here." Which was met with "Merry Christmas to you, too."

I began to wonder if we'd ended up in exactly the situation we had hoped to avoid by rejecting the offer of the venture capital firm: a large outside investor beginning to call the shots. It didn't help, not in the slightest, that the private label deal flopped like a big stinky beached whale on the rocky shores of our guayusa island.

The private label brand didn't sell as well as expected and was discontinued in short order, leaving us with pallets of unsold inventory that didn't even have our labels on it.

Welling up with increasing degrees of worry and anger, I decided to take up boxing to direct my restlessness somewhere else. The effort required by a two-hour workout left me gasping for air and temporarily blocked out the preoccupations that were beating me up all day, requiring me to access a more primal set of my survival instincts. And sadly, something about getting clocked while sparring and seeing stars for a brief moment gave me a reprieve from the more rooted pain and fear that seemed increasingly inescapable.

In order to keep things from further deteriorating, the board unanimously agreed that Runa would hire our mutual friend Rich Matusow, who was one of our investors and had been advising us informally for years. The idea was that he would work with us for several months to help figure out what the next stage of growth would look like and how to get everyone working together.

Rich was the perfect person for the job: he not only had deep experience building a brand that sold a product from the Amazon (açaí berries in the case of Sambazon) but was a dedicated yogi who has lived in ashrams off and on. Rich is very serene and even-keeled, giving him the ability to sit in a meeting, listen acutely without saying much, and at the end distill everything that was said down to a few key points and action items. Rich immediately helped to smooth things over, and it began to seem like we were back on track.

Meanwhile, I had been going back and forth with Costco in Northern California for months about testing Runa in their stores well before Rich came on board, and finalized a deal with them just after he started. I hadn't brought Rich into the conversation because I felt he was already inundated in his first few weeks. Moreover, I was excited to catch this big fish on my own and proudly bring it home as a symbol of my alpha status in the business. Pleased with my accomplishment and assuming the board would be ecstatic, I put it on the agenda for the next board call.

Rich, who had sold tens of millions of dollars to Costco while at Sambazon, was shocked I hadn't run the proposal by him before agreeing to it. "These are huge decisions with tricky margins," he said.

He ended up thinking the pricing and margins were too low. The board sided with him and rejected the deal despite Dan, Sara, and me all being in favor. I felt it was a huge mistake, and that a poor business decision was being made as a way to personally reprimand me for the communication breach. The board was angry with me for going solo and also faulted Dan for not keeping me "in line." There were so many bad feelings floating around that we had an emergency intervention and hired a $400-an-hour therapist to help us sort through things. It lasted for three hours and, in brief, did not go well for anyone but the therapist.

With nothing resolved, I had to go to Ecuador the next day for a handful of meetings, including one with the board of our subsidiary. We needed to approve a loan to expand our factory to meet increasing demand. We now had a representative from the Ecuadorian government on the board after the investment we took from them.

The loan had extremely favorable terms to us, given that it was coming from an impact-oriented family office, and it seemed like a no-brainer to approve. As the vote went around to the ministry representative—they sent a different low-level representative to each meeting—he read verbatim an unnecessarily long two-paragraph response that basically restated the proposal in flowery language.

The rest of us looked at each other, confused, and after a few seconds our lawyer asked him, "So are you voting yes or are you voting no?" He looked at her, then looked back down at the paper, and reread the verbose statement. After more silence and confused looks among the group, she asked, "Soooo you're voting . . . no?"

"No, no we're definitely not voting no," he said emphatically.

"Oh, OK. So you're voting yes, then?"

"No, no we definitely are not voting yes," he replied decisively.

"Ohhh-kaaay. So . . . you're abstaining?"

"No, we are not abstaining either."

"So let me get this straight. Here is what I'm going to write down in the meeting minutes. You are not voting yes, you are not voting no, AND you are not abstaining. Did I get that right?"

"Correct."

I had recently watched the movie *Birdman* and begun to feel exactly like Riggan, the character played by Michael Keaton, when shit really started to hit the fan and he, increasingly deranged, spiels to his daughter, "I'm not sleeping, like, you know, at all. And, um, this play [Runa in my case] is kinda starting to feel like a major deformed version of myself that just keeps following me around, hitting me in the balls with a tiny little hammer."

The day before coming back I got an urgent email saying "We need to talk ASAP." Our CFO was tasked with pre-notifying me that, after a string of closed-door meetings without Dan and me, the board's general consensus was that I needed to be fired. I had now run out of rope, my entrepreneurial lifeline cut short. There was going to be another emergency board meeting the next day at noon, she said, a few hours after my red-eye landed.

Engaging in an ancient practice more primordial than shamanism itself, I collapsed on the floor and started to cry hysterically. Not knowing what else to do, I called my parents, barely able to speak. As always, they bucked me up, simply telling me that they loved me and always would, no matter what happened.

It was easily the most broken I've ever been in my life. I couldn't get the thought out of my head: *I was getting kicked out of the company that I founded.* I felt like my child was being ripped from my arms.

On the way back up to Quito from the jungle, I stopped at some hot springs to try to relax before heading to the airport. As I sat in the baths, I smoked a fully packed pipe of *mapacho* and prayed hard for strength and trust, but just felt needles in my nerves and almost passed out.

I laid my pipe down and floated in the water. *Wow, this is it. I'm done,* I thought.

I noticed that the knot I'd had in my stomach for months momentarily unclenched. As I sat there, feeling calmer, I realized, *I'll just tell them I quit. I don't want to deal with this. If I don't have trust and support, it's just not worth it. It's all going to be OK. It's all going to be OK. It's all going to be OK . . .*

Rock Bottom

The next morning I arrived back in the U.S. feeling ready to let it all go. I hoped Dan could handle everything on his own, although I knew his commitment was wearing thin. With me gone, I figured that being solo CEO would be an exciting breath of fresh air. He'd messaged me the night before and said it was critical for the two of us to speak alone before we went to the meeting, so we met up at our office.

He wasted no time getting to the point. "I'm leaving," he said. "I've been thinking about this for months and just wanted to find the right time to tell you. But with everything going on with the board, I realized that I needed to let you and them know today before, you know . . . other decisions are made. We've had a great run, and beyond all the current drama, I'm just ready for new things and to step out of being a beverage salesman."

I felt Dan's earnestness and understood that this wasn't a hasty decision on his part. His primary focus had become managing our sales team, and he realized that he didn't want to be a beverage salesman for the rest of his life.

Kudos to Dan for the vision and courage, but it certainly threw a wrench in my plans.

Utterly confounded about what to do at this point, I went to smoke another big pipe of *mapacho* in the alley behind our office (definitely not as nice as an Andean hot spring), making a feeble attempt to pray that whatever happened would be in the best interest of Runa. After letting my prayers go up with the smoke alongside the smell of rotting trash, and catching the slightest glimpse of hope, my confused feelings and pounding frustration quickly returned.

It was quite an achievement that the board meeting went even worse than the therapy session. Feelings of hurt on all sides translated into accusations, name-calling, and a fair amount of curse words flying across the table.

Thankfully, Dan stepped in before it could degenerate any further.

"Guys! Guys! Calm down!" he said. "Runa is too special for this. It's way more important than your egos. I need to share about where I am before this goes too far."

Dan dropped his news. Silence.

Everyone immediately recognized that both cofounders leaving, by choice or by force, was going to be bad any which way you cut it. Without much more to discuss, the meeting broke up and we all went our separate ways.

That night, I left my phone in my apartment in Fort Greene and walked for hours and hours by myself through the streets and parks of Brooklyn. I was going to have to go back to some serious basics to get my head straight this time, and moving my body and getting some space hadn't failed me up to this point in the journey.

Drifting along the waterfront in the DUMBO neighborhood, I looked over the East River to the skyline of Lower Manhattan. I sat on a bench and closed my eyes, taking some deep breaths in an attempt to sooth my nerves. Soon an intense heaviness overcame my legs and stomach, making me feel like I would fall right through the bench.

My eyelids fluttered and I felt tingles on the back of my neck that gave me chills. The weight in my body started to loosen and release, like the ropes tethering a ship being untied and dropped onto a dock. I started to hum to myself in Shipibo, the words coming to me without thinking, with the phrase *Churo churo vainkin. Churo churo shamankin* looping back and forth with particular resonance.

I'm not sure how long that went on for, but at some point I

snapped out of it and leapt to my feet, startled that I had basically passed out by myself on a park bench at night.

Sitting back down, I noticed that I felt lighter. Returning to my contemplation of what to do, the anger and sadness that had been fueling my thoughts seemed to have lost its grip. *Churo churo vainkin* echoed through my mind: *Unwinding, as the ancestors say, the unraveling is happening.*

A common refrain in Shipibo shamanic singing, *churo* means to untie a knot, to get a kink out, or to remove an impediment or something that holds you in its grip. *Yeah,* I thought, *I'll definitely take some of that.*

After a day in which I'd felt emotionally pummeled, I was grateful for a bit of breathing room. And with some precious space to reflect beyond my resentment and fear, I managed to take account of my own errors and assess what I truly wanted.

My first insight was that, yes, I was the one who had primarily been acting like a dick. Feeling attacked or undervalued in no way could justify the fact that I wasn't listening to those around me in the most basic ways. I wasn't doing my part to hold a space of collaboration. I had gotten caught up in the criticisms people had of me and stuck on the story I had about not being supported, but the core inspiration for the feedback from everyone around me was to simply ask me to grow and step up as a leader.

Too preoccupied with being defensive, I had failed to get this critical point. It was time to get a real dose of humility and actually serve the company *in the ways that it needed*, not *in the ways in which I was most comfortable.*

My mind tried to push back on this insight, reminding me, *But they wanted to kick you out of* your *company!*

At that moment an epiphany gripped me and I saw through the shadow: My *company? Since when was Runa ever* my *company?*

I'd been launched into Runa from the plant *dietas* I'd done in Peru and felt that the company was something I was tasked with responsibly stewarding into the world. If Runa actually "belonged" to anyone, it could only be the spirit of guayusa and the Kichwa people, I realized. When did I develop this notion that it was mine to possess and control?

I saw that this core fallacy led me to become increasingly overprotective and adamant that Runa operate according to *my* requirements, even as the company attracted more and more talented people who were drawn by the product and the mission. My job as CEO was to steer us all toward achieving the larger vision. In failing to see that my own egotistical demands and attachments to scrappy ways of doing things were not the most important thing, I had helped pull the mountain down on top of my own head.

From Entrepreneur to CEO

The next day Rich and I sat down and had a meeting that, looking back at it now, seems quite magical. I articulated my newfound vision, apologized for missing the point of the board's prior feedback, and said that I was ready to step up to the plate if they wanted me to continue as the leader of the company. Thankfully, Rich had come to a similar perspective on his own, having told the board that *if* I could come around to a place of humility and openness, he would take on the responsibility of training me how to be the leader the company needed. Of course, the board thought he was being overly optimistic that I would actually welcome this seismic shift, but for some reason, some way, somehow, on that dreary New York morning our intentions aligned.

Another board meeting the next day was filled with hope and cautious optimism that Rich and I would be successful in helping me transition from hustling like an entrepreneur to leading like a CEO. The immediacy of the radical shift we all made—from explosive anger one day to collaboration the next—felt classically shamanic in that things had to get to their worst before there could be a purging and catharsis and then a rebirth, which was what it felt like.

Rich and I began a series of intensive meetings to help me change my leadership style. He helped me see how different the role of leader and manager is from that of entrepreneur. While I'd understood this concept theoretically before and could apply it to other people, I had arrogantly overlooked applying it to myself. *I'm not a business guy in the first place, so it doesn't apply to me,* I thought. *I just hustle and listen to the plants; that's what I do.* But it wasn't my job anymore to hustle nonstop and think that I had to do everything on my own. That was fine when it was just Dan and me, but it doesn't work when your primary job is setting the pace for the organization as a whole. In the world of boxing they say "Speed is rhythm and rhythm is speed," recognizing that rushing and lack of coordination only ends up slowing you down.

In business terms, Rich explained that we needed to shift from acting opportunistically to planning strategically. In the old world order of Runa, I had major FOMO ("fear of missing out") and jumped on every single opportunity with the hope that something would stick: a private label when we weren't ready for it, Costco when we hadn't thought it through, etc., etc. I'm convinced that, at least in part, this grit and tenacity provided us the steam we needed to get Runa off the ground. Our survival instincts were critical and we had the energy to work nonstop, even if we got little juice from the squeeze.

Rich wasn't against being opportunistic but recognized that you can be effectively opportunistic only when you have a clear strategy that is agreed upon and followed from the top to the bottom of the organization. With clear strategic goals, it becomes easy to evaluate opportunities based on whether or not they accomplish the main strategic priorities. In naïvely thinking that "growth" was the strategy, I saw every opportunity as relevant and useful. But growth was the goal, not the strategy.

I was pleasantly surprised to see how easy it became to see the need for turning down the majority of exciting, shiny new opportunities based on our new way of evaluating each one against the strategic priorities. I can't say it didn't feel uncomfortable turning them down at first, but ultimately this practice meant that we could capitalize on those *right* opportunities when they came, because we weren't distracted and overextended chasing the wrong ones.

I also went back to our tried-and-tested liberal arts strategy for business, and spent time interviewing other CEOs I admired about how to effectively lead an organization. The most singularly helpful piece of advice I received came from Blair Kellison, the CEO of Traditional Medicinals tea company.

He told me that as CEO you have to trust that your team members know how to do their jobs better than you do. If not, you hired the wrong people, and assembling the right team needs to be your highest priority. Once you have the right team, your job is to set the vision of where to go and clear obstacles out of the way, laying the path for them to move forward.

"Clear roadblocks and lay track," Blair said. "Those are the two things you have to do as CEO. That's it."

I began to realize how much being a successful CEO requires the opposite mind-set from that of a start-up entrepreneur. It isn't about how fast *you* can run, how many hurdles *you* can leap, or how many impossible challenges *you* can overcome. It is, rather, about enabling *others* to achieve those qualities in themselves.

In the world of shamanism, I've come to see a direct corollary. The "core technology" in the Shipibo tradition of doing *dietas* is the exact same for patients who need healing and for apprentices working to become healers. The basic logic is that in shamanic healing where "medicine" in the truest sense of the word is used, the primary goal and the primary effect is developing people's capacity to heal themselves. The core function of the shaman is to facilitate, with the plant teachers as the guides.

I'm deeply grateful that this brutal process granted me the opportunity to make progress on my own spectrum of healing and growth—healing from my own youthful ignorance, arrogance, and fears of being misunderstood, and growing into a space of more committed service and humility. These experiences of going past our "edges" most accurately convey the meaning of "shamanic." It is in moving through extremes, going to the far reaches of possibility, that life becomes most vivid, and our patterns and weaknesses are laid bare before us.

Chapter 12

Rooting Down and Growing Up

There is a shamanic concept that, when a physical body dies, the soul transmigrates into a new one, like the flame of a dying candle lighting another. The flame contains the essence of the former, but it gives life to something new, so it contains the previous life while embarking on its own journey.

In the aftermath of "Runa Implosion 2014," it seemed like this was happening within the company: virtually every facet of our business underwent a transformation that felt nothing short of a reincarnation. I certainly felt part of me had died and come back, and the taste of a new life was exhilarating.

The most symbolic manifestation of this reincarnation was

the redesigning of our labels. Dan and I had always been unhappy with the generic look of the Runa bottles and cans but had lived with the design in order to get the product on shelves. As time passed, we discovered that our growth and success were due primarily to people loving what was inside the bottle: the flavor and the energy. However, our labels were often driving away potential customers! This was the complete opposite of how beverage brands are supposed to work: the idea is to get you hyped up on brilliant marketing and clever design to cover up the fact the beverage, in most cases, is just sugar water.

One of my favorite examples of bullshit beverage marketing is when Vitaminwater got sued for making unwarranted health claims. The official defense from Coca-Cola, which had acquired Vitaminwater for $4.1 billion, was that "no consumer could reasonably be misled into thinking Vitaminwater was a healthy beverage." Right? I mean, who would think that products with the word "vitamin" in the name and drinks called Revive, Defense, and Endurance were actually healthy?

As Runa grew, we actively sought out feedback from store managers who tried to sell our products to their customers but failed to generate interest. We learned a lot when we asked why they thought the demand wasn't there. Some said, "It just looks like natural tea and doesn't come across as that unique"—in other words, the feel of the brand was completely failing to show our "dramatic difference." Other managers focused more on the basic communication: "People don't know what the heck it is. The fruit images make it look like juice, the word 'energy' on the bottles scares people off and makes them think of Red Bull, and you don't even use the word 'tea' on your freaking iced tea labels. People have no idea what you're selling."

Though some of our investors told us that changing our labels was incredibly risky, we knew that we could do better and started the process of redesigning them. An exhaustive search for a design agency ultimately lead us to Vault49, a funky crew of hipster Brits in the Flatiron district of Manhattan. Among all the core business challenges we've faced to make Runa a reality, I maintain that having to distill the entirety of our story, flavor, energy, and sustainability onto a two-by-three-inch space on the front of a bottle is at the top of the list.

We agreed early on that capturing all the aspects of Runa on a label would be impossible. So, rather than being literal, we had to be, first and foremost, evocative: the labels would have to convey the *feeling* of what we stand for.

We went through literally hundreds of designs that missed the mark in one way or another, started back from scratch multiple times, and came to within an inch of pulling the plug on the entire project and accepting that we would just never get there. We persevered, though, and finally emerged with labels that immediately got the "That's it!" response from our team and customers.

Using "Journey and Discovery" as our main design concept, Vault49 created a landscape silhouette on the bottle as a nod to the Amazon River itself. Curving up through the design, it can be seen both literally, as the river, or metaphorically, as an abstract pathway, leading to somewhere unknown. Everyone is invited to interpret it in their own way, and *relate* to the product as it supports their own journey.

With the energy cans, we embraced a more stripped-back aesthetic, using a leaf-like texture in the word "RUNA" to evoke discovery and spirited energy. We saw that, since competing energy drinks tend to go for a "More is more" aesthetic, we could stand out by refusing to shout.

Seeing the spirit of our mission reflected in our labels felt like the finishing touch on reinvigorating our principles, both grounding us and giving us the ability to sprout new branches as our roots sunk deeper.

Define Your Own Ceremony

During our early days in Ecuador, the local Kichwa leader would kick off each community meeting with up to forty-five minutes of repetitive facts that everyone seemed to know already. He talked about how their community was founded, how each person at the meeting had been invited, he repeated what the intention of the meeting would be, and on and on. When I eventually asked one community leader why he felt the need to do this, his response was: "If we don't know where we've come from, how can we find a way forward?"

Much later, Dan and I realized the value of these ceremonies. When we started building the beverage company part of Runa in New York, thousands of miles away from the Amazon, we wanted to include some of the Kichwa tradition to stay true to the roots of guayusa. We discovered two practices in particular that were inspired by our Kichwa brothers and sisters, but also relevant to our North American team.

First, we start each team meeting with "popcorn appreciations." One team member starts by relating a "High" (something good that is happening in their personal life, NOT related to work), and a "Low" (something challenging in their personal life). That person then chooses another team member in the circle and recognizes him/her for some way that he or she recently made a special contribution to the team. The person who was recognized relates his/her own High and Low, and then recognizes someone else. We continue until the circle gets completed and everyone has been recognized. The tone of positivity, support, and shared humanity that results from this simple practice is always palpable.

Another company policy we created is every Runa employee who works for us in the U.S. gets a fully paid trip to Ecuador on their one-year anniversary with Runa. By rewarding the hard work of each team member with a personal connection back to our company's roots, they also see firsthand the impact of their work. That reinforces the spirit of exchange and collaboration that is fundamental to guayusa.

Including these ceremonial elements in our business helps us to acknowledge where we stand, give thanks for where we are, and acknowledge everyone's contributions. As our company grows, making sure to maintain these ceremonial rituals means that the circle is always joined, and the founding intentions of the business remain a vital part of its future.

Expanding the Circle

My friend Denise introduced me to actress Olivia Wilde and her best friend, Babs Burchfield, who started Conscious Commerce together, an initiative whose mission is to integrate conscious consumerism into new markets and retailers. As part of their collaborations, they've created product lines with brands such as Anthropologie and Birchbox whose profits go to different partner nonprofits.

Olivia and Babs were tea fanatics and wanted to collaborate on a special Runa flavor to be co-branded with Conscious Commerce. When we met, Babs suggested mint and the night before I'd had a dream that I was walking beside a field of honeysuckle flowers, so within sixty seconds we came up with the idea for our Unsweetened Mint Honeysuckle flavor, which fit perfectly with our other top-selling flavors—a little out of the ordinary but not too crazy. They invested in Runa, we launched the flavor with great press coverage and social media support from Olivia, and within a few months it was one of our bestsellers.

We also formed a first-of-its-kind partnership with Leonardo DiCaprio, who decided to invest in Runa, join our advisory board, and then donate his shares to the indigenous communities in the Amazon.

Typically, investors make investments in companies, get some return, and then donate the profits to charities. DiCaprio's approach essentially cut out the intermediary step. By buying shares and then gifting them to the indigenous groups, he planted a seed of longer-term value in the communities' hands, where it would grow exponentially over time.

The day we announced the investment, Leo posted a beautiful picture of one of the Kichwa farmers on his social media channels, saying "Proud to invest in & join @DrinkRuna in supporting indigenous people of the Amazon whose futures are at risk as their native lands are exploited for natural resource and agricultural development . . . Empowering farmers like Maria [pictured on the Instagram] to stand up and fight back against the outside interests that threaten their survival is a cause that must be championed."

While there are numerous celebrity success stories in the beverage industry, such as 50 Cent profiting an estimated $100 million on his ownership stake in Vitaminwater, these deals are normally brokered with financial incentives at their core. I'd love to claim that Dan and I masterminded some ingenious strategy for attracting and persuading high-profile celebrities to support our mission, but the reality is far from it.

The leadership coach Simon Sinek says, "People don't buy what you do, they buy *why* you do it." Rather than paying celebrities to endorse our products, our authentic mission is what attracted each person to want to collaborate and be part of the journey with us.

Our community of high-profile investors has continued to grow in this spirit and now includes Marlon Wayans, Adam Rodriguez, and the professional tennis players Steve Johnson and John Isner. If these deals were brokered by anyone, I would have to say it was by the spirit of guayusa.

Trusting Guayusa

We learned during the rebranding process that the hours between 10:00 a.m. and 2:00 p.m. were the times when people really liked to hit the Runa—in other words, that window when you don't want to get too jittery from yet another cup of coffee but need something to fuel you through the rest of the day. It was a big open space in the category, given that most energy products focus heavily on nightlife and extreme sports.

Our newfound focus on this time led us to move beyond just selling to natural food and grocery stores. We expanded into colleges, starting with UMass, the University of Vermont, Brown, and Stanford, and also into corporate food service, landing Google, REI, Microsoft, and Amazon as early accounts.

We even began to receive some reports that we were outselling leading energy drink products on different campuses, and even replacing all other energy drinks in certain corporate cafeterias where employers wanted to steer their people away from artificial products. We also started receiving increasing amounts of positive feedback from consumers, who called guayusa everything from "Herbal Adderall" to "my Soul Cycle savior."

As the brand started to get traction, we faced a particularly challenging decision that hit right at the intersection of our mission and business interests: whether or not to sell guayusa as an ingredient to competitors. We were getting more and more inquiries from other companies that wanted to use guayusa in their own products, with no mention of Runa. As the only ones producing guayusa commercially, we could essentially decide whether they got it or not.

It was a difficult choice. We worried that by supplying other companies, we'd be inviting competition right next to us on the shelves and potentially hurt the sales of Runa products. On the other hand, wholesaling guayusa as an ingredient would bring more revenue, increase income for the farmers, and help grow awareness of the plant.

In the end, we went back to our foundational principle of the guayusa ceremony and asked ourselves: *WWGD—What would guayusa do?* The core intention of our business was not to be divisive and try to "control" everything but rather to follow the nature of guayusa itself. Beyond being a company, we felt responsible for stewarding the growth of guayusa as a nascent industry. We knew that the Kichwa believe guayusa to be incredibly beneficial to humans and that everyone, not just the indigenous groups, should drink it. We had to trust this core directive beyond any attempts to selfishly control the market.

We also figured that having more guayusa brewing in the kettle could only be a good thing and that if we sold guayusa to another company that ended up beating us at our own game, then we messed up. We now supply companies like Mamma Chia (which uses guayusa in their Chia Energy line), Juice Press (in drinks including their "Rocket Fuel" blend), and DAVIDsTEA, the largest tea retail chain in Canada, which sells guayusa straight and in blends.

The principle of strength in diversity that we learned from the Kichwa forest gardens where guayusa is grown applies here, too. Having a diversity of revenue sources—including loose leaf tea, bottles of tea, cans of energy drink, and guayusa wholesaling—gives our business core strength and adaptability.

Bringing Amazonian Plant Medicine to the World

When I visited the Sápara people in Ecuador with Channing and Reid, Manari Ushigua, the leader of the community, told us that he'd treated Westerners who had traveled to the jungle looking for cures to seemingly incurable diseases. With oil companies encroaching farther and farther into Sápara territory, Manari related a powerful realization of his own, one that I'm sure few of us would come to with such generosity: "Even if my people disappear, I see that it's critical we leave behind our knowledge of plants as a service to humanity."

He thought there might be a chance of saving the tribe if they could show they held something of more value to the world than barrels of oil, and he told us he wanted to start a clinic in the village.

From my perspective, the only powerful enough force that can offer an alternative, or even a meaningful complement, to extractive industries and destructive agriculture in the Amazon is medicine. Unfortunately, issues like climate change and deforestation lack urgency for most people. However, when you or someone you love is sick, then finding a cure becomes the most important thing in your life.

During my time in the Amazon, I met dozens of people who were seemingly cured of really tough addictions or autoimmune problems such as Graves' disease, Hashimoto's disease, and lupus after—in a very risky, last-ditch effort—they went to some hut in the jungle to receive traditional treatment.

If we could somehow clinically prove the efficacy of plant medicine treatments for modern diseases that Western medicine cannot effectively understand, let alone cure, what would the potential impacts be on environmental conservation efforts and cultural preservation programs?

An estimated 25 percent of modern drugs have been derived from rainforest plants, but less than 1 percent of the tropical plants in the world have been analyzed for their medicinal properties. With some fifty thousand plant species, is the Amazon not the forgotten bio-pharmacy of our species?

The thought in the West has been that when you find a plant

that has medicinal properties, you take it to a lab, isolate the active compounds, and concentrate them in a pill. However, there is a growing understanding that plants have incredibly complicated molecular structures fine-tuned by millions of years of evolution. When you alter and degrade that structure in a lab, you may lose part of its healing power.

The problem is that the effectiveness of Amazonian plant medicine has always been anecdotal and, to further the challenge, has never been documented or systematized in writing, unlike other ancient holistic medical systems such as Ayurveda in India and Chinese medicine. One way to change that, we realized, would be to use Amazonian medicine in a clinical setting, where the outcomes could be observed by Western researchers.

We decided to try that by building a rustic clinic in Sápara territory where patients would go to receive treatment for issues ranging from anxiety to depression to insomnia. The pieces almost magically fell into place. Channing and Reid immediately came on board to advise on the project and help raise funds. We quickly built a powerhouse advisory board, including Dr. Andrew Weil as well as physicians from Yale and Stanford.

In October 2016, we finished construction on the NAKU clinic, which is staffed by Sápara healers who will work with a rotating team of Western medical practitioners. Of course, we're still in the very early stages and it will take many years, if not decades, to reach any scientifically meaningful answers, but the vision taps into my passion so directly that I can see myself dedicating a substantial portion of my remaining years to this mission.

Finding a Path Where None Exists

On a recent trip down to Ecuador, I decided to attend a Saturday afternoon meeting of farmers and indigenous leaders at the border of Napo and Pastaza to drink *chicha*, get a feel for the cooperative's development, and enjoy the beauty of this scenic area. I rode one of our company motorcycles from Archidona through Tena and down to Puyo, a lovely route with sweeping views of the jungle and gorgeous turns on a perfectly paved road. From Puyo, I headed up the mountain and bounced over a terribly rocky road for almost two hours before reaching the community.

After three hours of blaring cumbia music, many conversations about Fair Trade Social Premium funds, a ritual of indigenous leaders squirting hot pepper juice in each other's eyes as a show of their strength, a few bowls of *chicha*, and many cups of iced guayusa later, I got ready to leave.

Hoping to avoid the long ride back to Puyo and then up through Tena and on to Archidona, I asked one of the women in the community if there was a more direct route.

"*Sí, sí*," she said. "Go up that road for a ways, make a left, then a right, then a left, then you get to the river with a bridge and you get to the road just below Tena."

Phew! That would save me hours. I tried to corroborate the instructions with a few different people to make sure I didn't get lost.

A younger man in the community answered my question by saying "*Sí, sí,* you can get direct to Tena from here. You go up that road for a ways, make a right, then another right, then two lefts and you hit the river and there is a boat that takes you over the river."

Hmmm . . . well, it sounded like there was a way, and I was game to figure it out as I went. The road was unbelievably rough and my bones shook as I banged along for two hours. I took a few wrong turns but was able to follow the topography of the mountain, with occasional views of the rivers below, so that I felt like I was keeping course.

Finally, I arrived at a river about sixty feet wide and the road stopped. I made it! I got off the bike, my skin still buzzing, and looked around for a bridge. Definitely no bridge. I couldn't see any huts or farms or people nearby either. Shit, no boat. But, squinting to look farther downriver, I caught a glimpse of the very top of a thatched roof hut on the other side.

I left the bike, stripped down to my underwear, and swam across with the mild current carrying me down as I went. A bewildered teenager stared at me as I emerged from the water, and was startled by my greeting of *Ali chishi* ("Good afternoon" in Kichwa). I told him my situation and asked if there was in fact a boat that could take me and my motorcycle across, to which he responded, "Yeah, my uncle's boat. I'll go get him and we'll meet you back across the river."

Victory, I thought! Ecstatic, I swam back across the river and watched the sky light up in violent purples and muted orange streaks as the sun set over the jungle. The air cooled and the birds sang. This was my bliss.

About thirty minutes later, I looked downriver and saw a twelve-foot-long dugout canoe turn the bend with the uncle pushing it through the current with a long stick.

OK, so that's the boat . . .

Without saying a word, we all stared at the canoe, then at the motorcycle, and back and forth for a few minutes, assessing if there was any way to make this work. Since the boat was only one foot wide, the bike would barely fit in the first place, regardless of the "to float or not to float" question.

Shuddering at the thought of riding back four hours on that horrible road in the dark, and then two hours back up on the main road, I decided to give it a go. The three of us lifted the bike into the canoe, which submerged in the water so that less than two inches remained between the side of the boat and the top of the water. With the teenager and me standing at the front and back to balance it, and the uncle at the rear pushing with the pole, we slowly set out.

Utterly focused, breath by breath, not a soul around to witness the absurdity, we progressed ten feet without an issue, another twenty, and another ten. We were almost across when a slight wobble sent us rocking and water began to slip over the edge. Somehow, the canoe steadied again and we eked out the last few feet to the shore and lifted out the bike.

We all started to laugh uproariously and exchanged big hugs—no need for commentary to spoil the moment.

The journey felt exactly like the one we've had since the very beginning of Runa. A little stupidity and a little ingenuity. Some lack of planning mixed with the excitement of not knowing but venturing off anyway. Some friendly, unexpected help from bemused locals turned friends. Moments of mounting fear and others of sublime beauty. All while floating between one bank and the next, centimeters away from complete inundation.

Conclusion

Give Thanks to the Wind

I used to think there would be a point where I would have the definitive answers. I craved that so badly—I would have traded in my own skin for something more secure if it could have only soothed my doubts and eliminated my own questioning, once and for all.

If I could somehow become "fully alive," *then* could I have full control? Not be subject to the pain, the sorrows, the self-doubt, but Transcend it (with a capital *T*!)—be in a state of perfect grace, peace, and tranquility all the time?

When I first set out on a shamanic path, I became confused as to why my quest to be "spiritual" and live in a principled way seemed to *increase* the amount of grief, sorrow, pain, and sadness I felt. Wasn't that the exact opposite of what I wanted?

I've had to learn, time and time again, the basic, inescapable order of operations programmed into the core of these practices: "Red man medicine makes you feel bad, then it makes you feel good." True power and fulfillment always seem to live behind the moat of the shadow. This is not "bad" or "unfortunate"; it's a gift.

Among the many master plants used for *dietas* in the Amazon, the big trees captivate a particularly high degree of reverence and respect from the elder shamans, who aim to learn from their simple, basic example: Grow your roots down deep. Reach up toward the light. Be strong so that you can support other life that will grow on and around you. Give thanks to the wind.

Most of that sounds cool and generically inspirational, I suppose, but giving thanks to the wind? If trees are grown in greenhouses with no wind, once they reach a certain height, they begin to tip over and hang limply. Having never faced any challenge to its growth, the tree never learns to resist and be strong. Standing up to the wind, however, requires the tree, no matter the degree of discomfort involved, to dig its roots down deeper and strengthen its core to resist the threat to its stability.

So give thanks to the wind, to the shadow, to that which challenges us, that which shows us where we are weak, that which *invites* us to be stronger. Our glorious burdens can become pearls transforming from an invasive parasite into a wonder of iridescent beauty. If I hadn't felt incomplete, anxious, and depressed, I never would have gone to the Amazon in the first place.

One of my favorite poets, David Whyte, vividly captures this sentiment in his book *The Heart Aroused:*

> It is as if we first stumble into our belonging by realizing how desperately out of place we feel . . . We might at first

label the body's simple need to focus inward depression. But as we practice going inward, we come to realize that much of it is not depression in the least; it is a cry for something else, often the physical body's simple need for rest, for contemplation, and for a kind of forgotten courage, one difficult to hear, demanding not a raise, but another life.

It seems that to find the real path we have to go *off* the path we are now on, even for an instant, and earn the privilege of losing our way.

In the world of shamanism, the pervasive archetype of the "wounded healer" arises from this core value of recognizing the gifts hidden in events that at first seem shattering.

Children who were hit by lightning, bitten by venomous snakes, or overtaken by life-threatening illness and survived became the healers. One could say they had some magical power or some miraculous gift that carried them through, making them destined to share this gift with others. Yet the way I see it, in more practical and simple terms, is that they accepted the invitation. They developed an intimate relationship with struggle, with "poison," which forced them to forge an even *deeper* relationship with life, with medicine, to survive. I can't remember which of the shamans I met said this, but it has always stuck with me. He said, "I don't have supernatural powers; I have natural powers that are super."

In the modern world, it's difficult to find even a single story of a respectable, honorable leader who wasn't accosted by adversity *and chose to listen*, who exchanged vows with the winds. These men and women show that pain, suffering, and hardship are not the enemies. Delusion, ignorance, and fear are the enemies.

This path of shamanism resonated with me because it is no more, and certainly no less, than a personal, empirical search for these deeper layers of life. These practices attracted me precisely because they were *not* prescriptive—in other words, it isn't *Do X and Y is going to happen.* The shamanic approach says, *Try X and see what happens for yourself. If you decide it's useful, then great. If not, fuck it, try Y.*

In that vein of thinking, I very much hope that your main takeaway isn't that everyone should go and find a shaman or start a business. While I feel the potency and sophistication of Amazonian plant medicines can have a powerful role to play in supporting humans through a dire and confusing period in both our personal and collective evolution, I implore anyone who approaches these plants and traditions to do so with extreme care and definite caution.

Do not check your skepticism at the door, humbly recognize your own limitations, and never let go of your own integrity. Vivid experiences and interactions with deeper layers of life and visionary states can be useful, for sure, but if "spiritual" experiences are not integrated toward the goal of you showing up with respect, honesty, compassion, and a commitment to service in everyday life, they have absolutely no value. Period.

Moreover, outside of the practical tools I've described to help you navigate difficult situations and explore your own potential, my deepest goal in revealing my experiences and understanding with Amazonian plants has not been to simply speak about this tradition itself but to use it to raise questions about the traditions of modern life more broadly. I firmly believe that our current definition of what it means to be human and what it means to do work in the world are decidedly constricted. I hope my story is just one of many more examples of how to approach this root question of what it means to be alive, and how we can work together to create a future that is fulfilling and healthy for all communities.

My hope is that you will trust your own intuition to venture where maps might not take you and see what's there for yourself. And as much as you might fight it, your fears and that which you resist are probably a great place to start that journey.

Even then, the anxieties never seem to go away, just like the wind won't ever stop blowing. On the Runa front, we are still a young company and will need to navigate the endless difficulties ahead as an unavoidable part of our growth process. Failure and struggle have been part of the deal, and I don't expect that to change. Sometimes it's sunny. Sometimes the rain pours down. My basic practices of meditation, praying with tobacco, attending ceremonies, and exercising have become the pillars of strength that help me dance with the wind. But I confess that I still fall into holes of depression as well. I still get woken up in the middle of night from terrifying nightmares, and I frequently forget to do, or consciously ignore, the daily practices I just listed so proudly. The reality of this constant failure generates the foundation of the most important practice of all: humility.

In the path of the wounded healer, rather than resist the feelings of depression or grief that arise and sometimes overcome me, I embrace them as best as I can. Saying yes to the fears when they come up, agreeing and validating the feelings of confusion and anger that come with the pervasive pain in the world, and being grateful for the simple ability to *feel* has transformed something that was once dreaded into a teacher.

Admittedly, sometimes my methods for embracing these

feelings come in the form of a cheeseburger and a movie, because it can't be "all spirituality all the time." The fullness of life as it is actually lived doesn't always happen there.

I deeply believe in this advice from my grandfather, which, in my view, represents the essence of what I feel all business worth the energy of the human spirit should aim to do: "Always work to uphold the highest ideals, and always be willing to compromise in service of those ideals."

It is through this intention of collaboration, when compromise is present, that we become fully alive with "both feet in both worlds." As Runa has grown, we've strived to build this into our business in every way we can. For example, after we go through our thirty-two-step process for properly packing, sealing, and documenting each sack of dried guayusa leaves at our factory in Ecuador before export, including application of specially coded holographic metal seals to each bag in accordance with NIMF code no. 15 and FDA Phytosanitary requirements, etc., we have one of the Kichwa elders come and bless each pallet and each container with guayusa and tobacco. I'm not sure the Kichwa have a traditional practice of "blessing pallets before putting them on a cargo boat for New York," but we're figuring it out as we go.

I strongly agree with the writer Elizabeth Gilbert, who points out that the advice to "follow your passion" leads to a certain amount of pressure and heaviness. The *expectation* that fully formed flowers will appear out of nowhere is, quite literally, groundless. It's *seeds of curiosity* that can lead to flowers of passion.

"Following your curiosity might lead you to your passion or it might not," she says. "You might get nothing out of it all except a beautiful, long life where all you did was follow your gorgeous curiosity."

I know for sure that I didn't start out feeling some burning passion about plants or business. I've grown to love both, but the initial spark was a curiosity and desire to at least acknowledge deeper parts of life that seemed ignored in the world around me. As you've seen, that questioning led to a very peculiar, roundabout path to the Amazon and eventually to Runa. Not everyone has a passion, but almost all of us have a few things we're curious about. The real battle, then, is making sure you make the space to listen to and follow those threads, wherever they may lead you.

Additional Information

Visit TylerGage.com/BookUnlock to:

- Read a bonus chapter
- See photographs and videos from the field
- Subscribe to learn more insider tips
- Learn additional exercises and tools
- Access exclusive interviews
- Direct any questions directly to the author
- Bring the author to your event

To contact Tyler directly, please email TG@tylergage.com.

Acknowledgments

To all the indigenous people whose words and traditions I relate, I acknowledge that I am a guest in your house and thank you for the incredible generosity you have shown me. If I have misinterpreted anything I sincerely apologize and ask for forgiveness. I give special thanks to the Kichwa and Shipibo families who have welcomed me into their homes and their hearts.

My fellow Runa cofounders, Dan MacCombie and Charlie Harding, deserve tremendous recognition, as our business exists out of the shared vision and hard work that we contributed together. Special thanks and recognition to Dan for hauling with me side by side for so many years, and for his rooted values, faith in humanity, and for dealing with my endless insanity at every turn.

My wife, Michelle, was my muse, main reviewer, sanity checker, and loving nourisher through the process of writing this book. She not only dealt with me going to the office at

4:30 a.m. to write before I had to start answering emails, but also with having yet another project that took my attention in the same year that we got married and moved across the country. Your love is my greatest inspiration.

My parents, Roger and Carolee, and my sister, Lindsay, gave me endless encouragement and feedback throughout the process as well, and I'm deeply grateful for their loving support no matter the degree of strangeness my journey takes on.

My agent, Zoë Pagnamenta, was a great shepherd for me as a total rookie in the book world, and it couldn't have felt more rewarding to work with Johanna Castillo as my editor. I'm deeply grateful to Johanna for recognizing the value of this story that shares the beauty of her homeland of Ecuador, and for believing in me. Enormous thanks to Doug Merlino as well for connecting to this story so deeply, for respecting the teachings of the indigenous people with such attention and depth, and for helping me weave the various threads of the narrative together. Thank you to my publicist, Kim Dower, and to the entire marketing and sales team at Atria Books and Simon & Schuster as well.

Thank you to my friends who took time to give me detailed feedback on versions of the manuscript: Nat Manning, Mary Wutz, Reid Carolin, Channing Tatum, and Tracey Merlino.

Everyone who has been a member of the Runa team in North and South America deserves tremendous credit for building the organization we have, and I wish I had the space here to name all of you. I would like to give special thanks and recognition to the leaders in our organization who have spent years working tirelessly with me and had particularly transformative effects on Runa up to this point: Sara Perkins, Dan

Segal, Eliot Logan-Hines, Francisco Mantilla, David Clark, Chris Kajander, Amelia Adler, Adriana Vinansaca, Jessica Dross, Katharine Attwell, Kavita Patel, Eddie Pearson, Eric Schnell, Richard Matusow, Luke Weil, Greg Robertson, Tammy Newmark, Mike Kirban, Bill Harrington, Leonardo Cerda, Alex Galindez, Fausto Garcia, Ian Cummins, Sydney Nilan, Aliana Piniero, Nick Olson, Manolo Samaniego, Gonzalo Torres, Silverio Mamallacta, Daniel Latacunga, and Aida Cardenas.

Props go to key members of our sales and marketing teams as well, who have done more to tell the story of Runa and share guayusa than I ever will: Alex Evans, Nick McCormick, Mike Murray, Dan Gold, Jimmy Christensen, Andy Ford, Dylan Van Buskirk, Jesse Hartheimer, Matthew Occelli, Oli Berlic, Lorenzo Lietti, Helene Rotolo, Walker Townsend, Dave Martin, Calvin Ross, Caroline Turnbull, Anna Premo, Demar Mills, Laura Homann, Andrew Gage, AJ Nocito, Angela Mohamed, Aaron Souza, Sol Tangvik, Zoe Liang, Tina Chu, and Sean Makau.

Endless gratitude to all our distributor and retail partners who proudly sell our products, with special gratitude to the team at Dora's Naturals in our hometown of New York City and also to Whole Foods Market for being the first ones to stock our products and for your continued support of our business.

Thank you to all my advisors and mentors, with special thanks to Tim Sullivan, Neil Kimberley, Mark Rampolla, Danny Warshay, Brian Krumrei, Alan Harlam, Bob Burke, Alan Sheriff, Winston Ibrahim, Ann Veneman, Yolanda Kakabadse, Matt Palevsky, Richard Perl, Didier Lacaze, Doug Hattaway, Tamara Newmoon, Arturo Izquierdo, Michael Ripley, Kip Roseman, and Jose, Lena, and Anna Stevens. You have all lit the way for me in magnificent and humbling ways.

I want to thank all the investors in Runa and donors to Runa Foundation who have quite literally made this dream possible.

Finally, thank you to everyone who drinks Runa and supports the farmers in Ecuador through your purchases. Knowing that you're out there always gives my heart a warm feeling. Thank you for picking up what we're throwing down.